HAUNTED DUNDEE

"Haunted Dundee — Book Two" was published by Langsyne Publishers Ltd, Old School, Blanefield, Glasgow in 1989 and printed by Waterside Printers at the same address.
Copyright Lang Syne Publishers Ltd 1989
ISBN: 185217 101 4

INTRODUCTION

- Leaders of the Black Band, a secret society of thugs who terrorised Dundee for 18 years, meet in their headquarters —the cellar of an Overgate slum. They are planning the latest in a series of robberies, assaults and burglaries.
- Two men found guilty of assaulting a young girl on the Dundee to Glamis road are whipped through the town. Each receives 13 lashes and will soon be shipped to a far-off penal colony to begin the main part of his sentence. It is 14 years hard labour each.
- In the eerie surroundings of the graveyard representatives of the nine trades meet and thereby carry on a curious tradition. They include the baker, shoemaker, glover, tailor, bonnet-maker, flesher, hammerman, weaver and the dyer.
- Although only four in the morning the piper o' the toun is marching through the streets playing on his bagpipe. This is the daily signal for folk to rise and shine and prepare for their chores. Later the bellman will go on his rounds making personal announcements on behalf of the townsfolk whilst all official proclamations will be made by the drummer.
- It is late in the evening and a river of bluish flame many yards wide rushes down Trades Lane towards Dock Street. A whisky bond's stores are on fire. The burning whisky, according to the local paper, "was a beautiful sight as it fell to the street in a variety of colours, sometimes purple, occasionally blue of different shades, and again red."

The full stories of these scenes and events are vividly portrayed by A.H.Miller in this second volume, which is a facsimile reprint from "Haunted Dundee."
Other stories feature:—
* The women who would be drowned if they ever set foot again in their home town.
* The witches, warlocks and demons of Claypotts Castle.
* Violence and murders most foul at the auld Dundee fairs which were supposed to be occasions of joy and pleasure.
* The amazing family Lamb who switched from being whisky and ale-sellers to temperance campaigners.
* The 'law woman' who made 'that muckle siller she was fear'd the Lord wad turn against her.'
* Mary Queen of Scots' Dundee letter summoning her people to war.
* Dramatic pleas for the execution of two 'spies' who are "come with an intention to murder all the men, to ravish all the women, and eat up all the children of Dundee."
* The eccentric characters who held the important post of town drummer over the years.
* The only occasion when tradesmen from other towns and villages could sell their wares in the streets of Dundee.

Down among the dead men — butcher, baker and bonnet-maker

WHEN the Trades Hall, which stood at the east end of the High Street on the site directly in front of the Clydesdale Bank, was opened in September, 1778, the Nine Trades were accommodated with separate chambers in the building. Previous to that time the Trades, from about 1580, were accustomed to meet for the disposal of business (the election of Deacons and of Town Councillors, and other matters connected with the Crafts) in the Howff, or Burial-ground of Dundee.

Usually each Craft selected a part of the cemetery where some notable member of the Craft lay buried. Thus the Bakers convened beside the grave of David Tendall, a famous Deacon in the sixteenth century; and the other Trades followed this quaint example, thus giving a sentimental aspect to the most prosaic business. It seemed as if the living members of the Craft were calling their dead brother to witness that they were upholding the dignity of the Trade with which he had been connected.

This curious custom continued until the Trades decided to combine so as to build a hall that would afford accommodation commensurate with the advance in social affairs. No longer was it convenient or dignified to hold meetings in the open air; and the Nine Incorporated Trades raised a joint fund to pay for a general meeting-place.

The building was designed by Samuel Bell, a famous local architect, who also provided the design for the English Episcopal Chapel at the west end of High Street, which afterwards became the Union Hall. Both these buildings were in keeping with the style of the Town House; and the High Street (the Market-gait of the olden days) had quite a Flemish appearance before these two halls were demolished.

The Nine Trades that erected the Trades Hall were the Bakers, Shoemakers, Glovers, Tailors, Bonnet-makers, Fleshers, Hammermen, Weavers, and Dyers, and their motto "Nine in One" was carved on the pediment of the hall, together with the arms of each separate Trade. The Trades Hall was opened in 1778 with a great display of magnificence, the Trades meeting in the Howff, and marching through the town in procession to take possession of the new premises.

The apartment occupied by the Shoemaker Craft in the Trades Hall was situated on the third flat, facing the Seagate. The separate chambers were allotted to the different Trades by ballot, and the Shoemakers (or Cordiners, as they were anciently designated) determined to decorate their place of meeting in a special manner. They engaged Mr Methven, a prominent decorator in Dundee, to paint a mural picture on the wall of the room, below the cornice, representing the Procession of King Crispin in Dundee.

This procession had at one time been an annual display, but had fallen into desuetude; and the Craft purposed to preserve a record of its days of former glory by keeping this picture perpetually before the members. The work was left incomplete by Mr. Methven, and remained unfinished for over forty years. At length, in 1822, the Craft employed Henry Harwood, a well known local artist, to complete the picture, and this was done forthwith.

This strange work of art is painted in oil-colours on the plaster. It represents the craftsmen who were associated with the Cordiner Trade, marching in a long procession, headed by the Earl Marshal on horseback; with the representative of King Crispin, royally robed, wearing a crown, and with four pages holding up his train; with the Champion on horseback, clad in armour; and with the craftsmen in knee-breeches, embroidered tailed-coats, cocked-hats, and all the splendour of holiday clothing of the most elaborate kind.

The Deacons and Past Deacons marched in the procession before the King, wearing white satin coats and breeches; and altogether the display was lavish and expensive, though possibly not impressive to the cynical spectator. Prominent land-marks such as the Auld Steeple and the Law Hill are brought into the picture, with the Tay in the distance. Though

THE CHAMPION & THE EARL MARSHAL

KING CRISPIN & HIS ATTENDANTS

"AULD MAHOUN" THE SARACEN

not a great work of art, this picture is extremely interesting as a relic of ancient burgh life.

The Trades Hall passed through many vicissitudes during its existence. The large central hall, which was only required for general meetings of the combined Trades, was frequently let for public meetings. At one time it was used as a Theatre; at another it was occupied as the Dundee Exchange Coffee-Rooms; and here many of the public banquets took place, so that it became an important centre of civic life. In 1850 the shops on the street floor were altered and enlarged to suit the progress of the time. The large hall was occupied by the Eastern Bank from 1838 till its amalgamation with the Clydesdale Bank in 1864, and its use as a bank was continued until the present building of the latter Company was completed.

At length, when the Improvement Act of 1878 came into force, the Trades Hall was acquired by the Town Council, and demolished to make way for the widening of the Murraygate. While the building was being removed, Mr. John MacLauchlan, the energetic Chief Librarian of the Dundee Free Library, called the attention of the Town Council to this mural picture, and on his initiative it was carefully cut out from the wall and placed in the Town House for preservation. Ultimately it was taken to the Albert Institute and put up in the main corridor, where it stood for several years. It has now been removed and placed, very appropriately, in the Picture Gallery in the Central Reading-Rooms, Ward Road, reserved for views of Old Dundee.

In pre-Reformation times it was customary for each of the separate Trades to have a Saint as protector. Thus St. Aubert was the patron Saint of the Bakers, St. Severus of the Weavers, St. Mark of the Walker (or Dyer) Craft, St. Duthac of the Glovers, St. Crispin of the Shoemakers; and from early records it is shown that there were altars or chaplainries dedicated to nearly all of these Saints in the Church of St. Mary of Dundee, which were maintained by the different Trades.

The exception was St. Crispin. There was no altar to this Saint in St. Mary's Church, and it is probable that the Cordiners contributed to the support of the Altar of Corpus Christi there, just as the Guildry was responsible for the expenses of "the Halie Bluid Altar." And thereby hangs a curious story, which shows how the old Roman Catholic ceremonies were preserved in an altered form after the Reformation. To understand this it is necessary to know the history of the Saint of the Cordiners' Craft.

In the Rev. Alban Butler's "Lives of the Fathers and Martyrs," the true story of St. Crispin and his brother St. Crispinian is thus related:—"The brothers came from Rome to preach the faith in Gaul towards the middle of the third century together with St. Quintin and others. Fixing their residence at Soissons, in imitation of St. Paul they instructed many in the faith of Christ, which they preached publicly in the day at seasonable times; and, in imitation of St. Paul, worked with their hands in the night, making shoes, though they are said to have been nobly born, and brothers. The infidels listened to their instructions, and were astonished at the example of their lives, especially of their charity, disinterestedness, heavenly piety, and contempt of glory and all earthly things; and the effect was the conversion of many to the Christian faith.

"The brothers had continued this employment several years, when the Emperor Maximian Herculeus coming into Belgic Gaul, a complaint was lodged against them. The Emperor, perhaps as much to gratify their accusers as to indulge his own superstition and give way to his savage cruelty, gave order that they should be convened before Rictius Varus, the most implacable enemy of the Christian name, whom he had first made Governor of that part of Gaul, and had then advanced to the dignity of Prefect of the Prætorium. The martyrs were victorious over this most inhuman judge by the patience and constancy with which they bore the most cruel torments, and finished their course by the sword about the year 287 A.D. They are mentioned in the Martyrologies of St. Jerome, Bede, Florus, Ado, Usuard, and others. A great church was built at Soissons in their honour in the sixth century, and St. Eligius richly ornamented their sacred shrine."

In all the Roman Catholic churches where there was an Altar of Corpus Christi it was usual to have a public procession through the streets of the city on the Thursday after Trinity Sunday. On this day the consecrated Host was carried with great pageantry, and the different Crafts took part in the parade. From an Inventory of the goods and ornaments in St. Mary's Church, Dundee, dated about 1454, it appears that the decorations for the Procession of Corpus Christi then consisted of the following articles:—

Twenty-three Crowns, seven pairs of angels' wings, three mitres, Christ's coat of leather, with the hose and gloves, Christ's head, thirty-one swords, three long crosses made of wood, St. Thomas's spear, a cross for St. Blaize, a cradle and three "bairns" made of cloth, twenty heads of hair (wigs), the four Evangelists, St. Catharine's Wheel, St. Andrew's Cross, a saw, an axe, a razor, a gully knife, a worm (serpent) made of wood, the Holy Lamb made of wool, St. Barball Castle and Abraham's hat. These details give some idea of the nature of the procession of Corpus Christi through Dundee in the fifteenth century.

It will be noticed that the emblems were representative of the principal Trades, and thus the ceremony was partly religious and partly secular. Though no specific record exists of this procession in Dundee, there can be no doubt that it was faithfully observed up till the time of the Reformation.

When the Protestant religion had gained a firm hold in Dundee—"the Geneva of Scotland," as it was called—this procession, of course, had to be discontinued; but the people, very naturally, were unwilling to lose a glorified holiday of this kind. They could not have a Procession of Corpus Christi, nor could they make a Saint's Day the excuse for such a display. The Shoemaker Craft here stepped forward to the rescue. Their Saint, as stated, was St. Crispin. The name was similar in sound to "Corpus Christi," the altar supported by the Craft; but then they dared not have a Procession of St. Crispin without offending the Protestant ministers. They therefore transformed "Saint Crispin" into "King Crispin," and thus, very simply, altered a religious ceremony into a secular parade, and kept their consciences clear.

St. Crispin's Day was thus observed in Dundee for over two hundred years. In 1783 it was celebrated with special magnificence; but for 39 years after that date there was no King Crispin Procession. In 1822 the visit of George IV. to Scotland had revived the taste for spectacular display; and the members of the Shoemaker Craft decided to revive the parade with which their Trade had been so long associated.

At noon on Wednesday, 2nd October, 1822, the Shoemakers of Dundee and the neighbourhood assembled in front of the Trades Hall, clad in all the mediæval trappings which formerly graced this display. The picture, of which three portions are here reproduced, shows the style adopted by the tradesmen and their officials. Starting from the east end of the High Street, the procession marched along the Nethergate, up Tay Street, eastward through the Overgate, Murraygate, and Cowgate, and back by the Seagate to the Trades Hall.

The "Dundee Advertiser" of 3rd October, 1822, thus records the incident:—"The rarity of the procession attracted the curious and the idle, and the High Street was crowded to excess for upwards of two hours. From the want of previous arrangement to keep off the excessive crowd, the procession advanced with difficulty and laboured hard, and only the equestrians, such as the Champion, the Earl Marshal, and a few other grandees were visible above the mass of heads. As the procession moved up the Overgate, a pedlar contrived to perch his person upon a table in front of his shop. But no sooner did His Mock Majesty appear than the table broke down, and the fall of the pedlar was construed into a profound reverence to Crispin."

Thus ended the reign of King Crispin in Dundee.

Inferno! Buried alive under burning bricks and blazing bales

A PROPOSAL was lately made to change the name of Trades Lane, and call the new continuous street from the Cowgate to Dock Street by the name of the upper portion—St. Andrew's Street. This notion was wisely abandoned, as it would have seriously perplexed the future historian of Dundee if the name of Trades Lane were wiped out entirely. That thoroughfare, though not one of the ancient streets of Dundee, and not much more than a century old, has figured prominently in civic affairs, and gained an unenviable notoriety for its conflagrations.

Three alarming fires occurred here during the past century, each more disastrous than its predecessor. The first of these took place in October, 1835, the second twenty years later, in June, 1855, and the latest and most pathetic in September, 1870, when two esteemed officials lost their lives. The story of these events will revive recollections of the two last-named disasters in the minds of the older generation of Dundonians.

Ninety years ago Trades Lane presented a very different appearance from that which it has to-day. The open field which is shown in Crawford's map of 1770 as extending from the Seagate to the river had been feued chiefly for works. On the east side of the thoroughfare, in 1835, Mr. Calman's shipbuilding yard was at the south, where Dock Street now has been reclaimed from the river. Further up the street were the engine works and foundry of Mr. Borrie, one of the pioneers of marine engineering.

The Trades Lane Calendering Co. had recently completed new premises at the corner of Seagate; and their former building—the scene of the disaster—lay between their new place and Mr. Borrie's works. At that time it was rented by Messrs. Guthrie & Baxter, and used as a store for hemp and codilla. The building where the fire occurred was thus surrounded by structures of a highly inflammable character. About half-past ten o'clock on the evening of Saturday, 31st October, 1835, smoke was observed issuing from the store, and the watchman of the First Ward speedily raised an alarm. The news of a fire in this thickly-populated district soon brought an immense crowd to the scene. Mr. Calman's carpenters, Mr. Borrie's engineers and foundry men, and the employees in the Trades Lane Calender, most of whom lived in the vicinity of these works, were attracted to the spot, and many of them lent active assistance in subduing the fire.

At that time the Dundee Fire Establishment had been quite recently organised. For several years before 1835, the "Dundee Advertiser" had been strongly advocating the establishment of a regular Fire Station, instead of trusting wholly to the imperfect means adopted by the Insurance Companies and by individual mill proprietors.

On Sunday, 16th January, 1835, a terrible conflagration took place in the warehouse belonging to Mr. James Watt in Dock Street, the store there containing about 300 tons of hemp and codilla and upwards of 300 barrels of tar. The fire was described as forming "a volcano," the tar soaking the hemp and blazing with terrible fury. Five men were killed by the falling of a gable. This incident compelled the Town Council to take action in forming a Fire Salvage Establishment, and, after much circumlocution, the Council, in conjunction with the Harbour Trustees, formulated a scheme and carried it out. In the "Dundee Advertiser" of 3rd April, 1835, the following paragraph describes the primitive Fire Brigade:—

"At last Dundee is on the eve of procuring a proper establishment for giving powerful aid in the extinction of fires. Mr. Matthew, Clerk of Works at the Harbour, has been appointed Superintendent of the Fire Corps. Twenty firemen have been appointed at present. A new fire engine of great power has been ordered, and other ten firemen will be appointed when it has been procured. The firemen are to be dressed in uniform, blue jackets and vests, canvas trousers no wider than is necessary for easy movement of the limbs, helmets strongly fortified to save the head in the midst of danger. The Fire Corps is to be regularly drilled in the necessary duties."

Such was the condition of the Dundee Fire Establishment when the first great Trades Lane fire broke out. It was supported by subscriptions from the Town Council, the Harbour Trustees, and the Fire Insurance Companies, and as the total sum gathered each year only amounted to £160, it soon fell into bankruptcy. But the Trades Lane fire of 1835 gave the first opportunity of showing the mettle of the Fire Brigade. The Hand-pumping Fire Engine used on this occasion is now obsolete, and is preserved at Dudhope Museum.

The Brigade was turned out under Captain Matthew, and many willing hands lent aid in the subjugation of the fire. It soon became evident that special efforts must be made if Mr. Borrie's works were to be saved. A band of firemen, assisted by Borrie's engineers, began to demolish the roofs of the sheds at the engine-works, while another band, with workers from the calender, strove to limit the conflagration by a similar method on the north.

As in the Great Fire of London, it was found necessary to circumscribe its area by making a blank space around it, and this plan proved successful. After a prolonged struggle, the "devouring element" was conquered, and the conflagration terminated without any tragic loss of life.

Within the next few years the Fire Brigade had many trying experiences at large factory fires. In June, 1836, the extensive engineering and foundry works of Messrs. Kinmond, Hutton, & Steele, at the Dens, were totally destroyed by fire. In October of the same year the new spinning mill of Mr. John Mitchell, at Polepark, was burned.

In August, 1840, the Brigade was perplexed by a double fire. Mr. Thoms' mill in Barrack Street was reported to be on fire, and while the firemen were there, a fresh alarm was raised that Mr. Lindsay's mill in Henderson's Wynd was in the same condition. This proved to be a dreadful conflagration. The building and machinery, which had cost over £20,000, were totally destroyed. On this occasion the Fire Brigade was assisted by the soldiers from the Barracks, under the command of Captain Beresford.

By a strange fatality, the fire which broke out in Trades Lane on the night of Tuesday, 5th June, 1855, involved some of the buildings which had been saved twenty years before. The portion of Mr. Borrie's foundry which had been erected about 1830 was then used as a series of stores for flax, and was occupied by Mr. Collier, Messrs. Paton & Fleming, Messrs. Neish & Small, and other merchants.

The buildings were situated between Trades Lane and Mary Ann Lane, and extended in the form of the letter H from a court near the Seagate on the north, to Dock Street on the south. The Trades Lane Calender was at the northern boundary, and thus the fire involved all the buildings in Trades Lane on the east side, except the Calender Works.

The first intimation of danger was the smoke which was seen issuing from the one-storey brick building occupied by Mr. Collier; and shortly afterwards there was a similar outbreak about 300 feet away from the spot first observed. The fire spread rapidly through all parts of the range, and soon the whole of the contiguous structures, holding over 1400 tons of flax, hemp, jute, etc., were one glowing mass of fire.

It was stated at the time that the reflection of this huge volume of flame was visible at Blairgowrie, at Perth, and at Edinburgh; while at Broughty Ferry it was possible to read the newspapers at midnight by this artificial light. The scene was thus graphically described by the reporter of the "Dundee Advertiser":—

"The view from the Nethergate was one of awful magnificence. The spire of St. Paul's Episcopal Church was brilliantly relieved from the intense light behind, and the houses around were lighted up with a lurid splendour almost surpassing the brightness of the noonday sun. The appearance of the burning mass itself was one of terrific grandeur. From the roofless warehouses and from the windows, as from the craters of volcanoes, issued streams of lurid flame, and portions of the walls, from the intense heat, which was felt at a great distance, were ever and anon falling amongst the flames, and causing clouds of fire-dust to ascend with spasmodic force, which, even in the calm atmosphere, were borne to a great distance from the scene of conflagration."

As on the previous occasion of a great fire, the soldiers in the Barracks turned out, and did much service, both in maintaining order and in helping the firemen. The fire continued to rage with great fury till long after midnight and not until two o'clock in the morning were there any signs of its abating. The loss was estimated at over £50,000. Mr. Fyffe was then in command of the Fire Brigade, and he was destined to meet his death at the same spot a few years later.

The terrible conflagration in Trades Lane, which took place on Sunday, 18th September, 1870, far transcended the others in its melancholy results. The warehouse belonging to Messrs. John Gordon & Co., linen manufacturers, stood on the east side of Trades Lane, and extended from about the middle of that thoroughfare southward to Dock Street. It was a one-storey building 300 feet long, 40 feet broad, and 16 feet high, the walls being of brick nine inches thick.

About midnight the policeman in Dock Street noticed smoke issuing from the south end of the building, and raised an alarm. The Fire Brigade under Captain Fyffe was soon at the scene, and about 50 men of the 90th Regiment came from the Barracks. The building was not divided by partitions, and there was thus no chance of localising the fire, as it was directly communicated from bale to bale of the 1500 tons of flax, codilla, tow, and jute, with which the store was packed. Almost from the first it was plain that none of the goods could be saved. Efforts were directed, therefore, to preventing the fire from spreading to the adjacent buildings.

On the east side of the burning warehouse there was a narrow lane, about nine feet wide. Captain Fyffe noticed that the door of Borrie's store at the head of this lane had caught fire, and he went thither, accompanied by six of his assistants, a large crowd of spectators following them.

The firemen had hardly begun to direct their hose upon the burning building when a fearful catastrophe took place. The action of the intense heat had so expanded the bales in the store that the nine-inch wall could not resist the pressure; and at once, without warning, the brickwork, about 30 feet long by 16 feet high, suddenly collapsed, the ruins falling upon the crowd in the narrow lane, and burying some of them beneath the burning bricks and the blazing bales. As the lane was not "through-going"—that is, had only one entrance and exit—those at the further end had no chance of escape, while the crowd at the southern portion of the lane could only save themselves by a stampede.

Dr. Charles Moon, who was present in the lane, exhibited

great courage, and repeatedly attempted to rescue those who were buried under the ruins. Nor for some time was it possible to bring out the dead and wounded from the fiery death-trap in which they had been caught. At length it was found that there were four killed and nine seriously injured. The dead were Captain James Fyffe, Superintendent of the Fire Brigade; Sergeant James Watson, Burgh Police; Robert Jenkins, fish-dealer, Blackness Road; and Bernard Clark, mill foreman to Messrs. Edward.

Captain Fyffe was originally a slater, but had been connected with the Fire Brigade for 35 years. He was 58 years of age, and was about to resign his office when death overtook him in the performance of his duty. Sergeant James Watson had been a member of the police force for over 20 years, and had risen to rank through his ability and trustworthiness. It was no part of his duty to be present at this fire; he was there as a volunteer. Both those victims of the fire were buried in the Western Cemetery on separate days, and a large concourse of the people attended their obsequies. Monuments to both of them were placed on their graves. The obelisk which marks the grave of Captain James Fyffe bears the following inscription:—

> Erected by the Commissioners of Police of the Burgh of Dundee, to the memory of JAMES FYFFE, Superintendent of the Dundee Fire Brigade, who discharged the responsible duties of that office during 25 years with energy, discretion, and judgment; and who died in the zealous performance of his public duty while endeavouring to extinguish a fire at a flax warehouse in Trades Lane, Dundee, on 18th September, 1870.

The inscription on Sergeant Watson's tombstone is in similar terms. The loss by this fire was estimated at about £40,000. Since that time Trades Lane has not been immune from fire, though stone-built premises have taken the place of the brick erections which once formed the east side of that thoroughfare.

In the early morning of Thursday, 9th July, 1891, the warehouse which had been built on the site of the one destroyed in 1870 was burned to the ground. It was then in the possession of Messrs. Fleming, Douglas, & Co., and was used for storing jute. The block was 120 feet of frontage, and extended 80 feet back from the street; and while the fire was in progress it was found necessary to pull down the front wall to prevent it from collapsing. Captain Ramsay had then charge of the Fire Brigade. The loss entailed amounted to £20,000, and the fire smouldered so long that the street was closed against traffic from Thursday till Saturday. A similar fate overtook the warehouse erected next to the calender, on Wednesday, 4th May, 1904, when the store belonging to Messrs T. S. Ross & Co. was totally destroyed, the loss being about £20,000. Clearly this side of Trades Lane had the shadow of disaster hanging over it for nearly a century.

By far the most destructive fire recorded in the history of Dundee took place in this locality on Thursday, 19th July, 1906, and raged for two days. It originated in the bonded stores of Messrs. James Watson & Co. Ltd., distillers. The premises comprised an imposing range of stone structures, three of which fronted Seagate, and three Trades Lane on the West side. These stores were six storeys high, and contained, it was computed, nearly a million gallons of spirits, principally whisky and rum. At the North-West corner of Trades Lane stood the establishment of the Scottish Co-operative Wholesale Society, a brick building two storeys in height, which contained extensive stores of provisions. On the North-East side of Trades Lane stood the Trades Lane Calendering Company's works; while on the North side of Seagate, opposite Messrs. Watson's establishment, were, extensive bonded stores of Messrs. John Robertson & Sons distillers, a large tenement property, and the offices of Mr. James Fairweather, tobacco manufacturer. It will thus be seen that the area contained highly inflammable material.

The fire began shortly after 6 p.m., when most of the staff had left, and smoke was noticed issuing from the roof of one of the largest bonded stores in Watson's building. The Fire Brigade, under Captain Weir, was speedily on the scene, but no one foresaw that this was the beginning of a terrible conflagration. It was soon apparent that the whole roof was ablaze, and the fire was rapidly descending to the lower flats. Sheets of flame, sometimes a hundred feet in extent, were blown by the Western breeze across Trades Lane, and the

HAUNTED DUNDEE VOL. 2   15

Terror of Claypotts!

Fleeing the flames!

Calender was only preserved from destruction by the workers, who kept pouring streams of water on the building.

About an hour after the fire began a terrible explosion occurred, caused by the ignition of the contents of a large vat containing about 1000 gallons of whisky. All the windows were blown out simultaneously in Seagate and Trades Lane, doing damage to the buildings on North side of Seagate, and making it necessary to remove all the residents in the tenement there. The following account is quoted from the "Dundee Advertiser":—

"A strange sight now arrested the attention of the spectators. The escaping spirits, percolating through the interstices of the gable, reached the outside, and, igniting, flowed down the wall, a stream of sulphuric flame. The scene at this stage was appalling, and positively baffled description. With a deep roar like the reverberations of Niagara, the flames leaped about their prey, licking the bare gaunt walls of the ruined warehouses, and threatening every minute to consume the others. . . . Slowly creeping to the utmost recesses of the building, the fire shortly after ten o'clock gained access to a large quantity of liquor housed in the south-west corner. As the bottles cracked and the casks burst, the liquor poured in large streams from many of the windows. The whisky, which was on fire, was a beautiful sight as it fell to the street in a variety of colours, sometimes purple, occasionally blue of different shades, and again red. A river of bluish flame, many yards in width, rushed down Trades Lane towards Dock Street, and the more the firemen drenched it with water, the keener it appeared to burn."

For some time it was thought that the Co-operative Store would escape; but when Watson's building in Trades Lane burst into flame about nine o'clock it was evident that the Store was doomed, and in less than half-an-hour it was reduced to ruins. On the West side of the narrow street called Candle Lane, to the West of Watson's main structure, there were whisky stores belonging to Messrs. John Robertson & Sons, and these also were soon destroyed. In Mary Ann Lane, which is east of Trades Lane, there were several large sheds containing bales of jute, and these were set on fire by blazing embers that had been thrown by explosions a long distance. The sheds were totally destroyed.

When the fire at Watson's had been partially subdued, steps had to be taken for the demolition of the lofty ruined walls, which were in a dangerous condition. This was no easy task, but it was safely accomplished under the direction of Mr. James Thomson, City Architect. For about three days the fire smouldered over this vast area, and many prodigies of valour were accomplished by the firemen, though no lives were lost. The value of the property destroyed is shown in the following table:—

Messrs. Watson,	£180,000
Messrs. Robertson,	70,000
T. S. Ross & Co.,	60,000
Messrs. Henderson,	20,000
Co-operative Society,	7,000
Stewart Robertson,	6,000
Trades Lane Calender,	5,000
Other losses,	42,000
	£400,000

Messrs. Watson, in 1908, erected a still finer building for their stores and offices upon the site of their former place thus made memorable.

Witches, warlocks and demons of Claypotts

THERE are few of the residents in Dundee and Broughty Ferry who do not know the quaint old structure of Claypotts Castle. Hardly one of the uninhabited castles in Scotland is so well preserved as this structure, though for many years it has been used principally as a store in connection with the farm.

It is nearly five centuries and a half since the existing building was erected; and very little expense would make it quite fit for habitation at the present day. It is built on what is known as the Z plan—that is, there is an oblong central building, and at the corners diagonally opposite there are large round towers, carried up from the ground, the top storey being corbelled out to form a square structure finished with crow-step gables.

The oblong keep measures 35 feet by 25 feet, and the circular towers are constructed on a radius of 11 feet, the main building being four storeys in height. Small circular towers with spiral staircases are placed at the points where the large round towers join the main building, and access is thus afforded to the upper flats.

The ground floor is very strongly built, the walls there being five feet thick, almost the only apertures for light consisting of narrow shot-holes suitable for firearms. The kitchen has been placed in one of the round towers, the other having been used as a store room. The roofs are vaulted, and the apartment in the oblong keep is divided by a partition to make two store rooms.

The hall, as usual, is on the first floor, and is a well-proportioned apartment, measuring 27 feet by 18 feet. A screen of some kind, either wood pannelling or tapestry, has extended across the hall from the staircase entrance to the opposite wall, the purpose being to permit of entrance from the stair to the ante-chamber thus formed, instead of passing directly from the staircase into the hall. Light is obtained from single windows in each of the three walls, and a private room in one of the large towers has an entrance from the hall. The floor of this splendid apartment is composed of pavement slabs that rest upon the vaulted roof beneath. The upper floors are of wood, now very much decayed.

At the exterior of the top flat, at the angles of the oblong keep opposite to those occupied by the round towers, there are battlements where sentries might be stationed on the lookout; this arrangement showing that the Castle was built at a time when the proprietor might be called upon to defend his habitation from the attacks of his enemies. The old roof-timbers still remain, and instead of slates, the flake stones are fixed to laths by wooden pins.

Despite the neglect with which it has been treated, this sturdy Castle seems likely to remain a monument of honest masonry when many a modern jerry-building will be reduced to the condition of "a shapeless cairn."

In ancient times the lands of Claypotts belonged to the Barony of Dundee, and thus came into the possession of the famous David, Earl of Huntingdon, when he obtained the burgh from his brother, William the Lion, towards the close of the twelfth century. Alexander II. gave the superiority of the lands to the Abbey of Lindores, and this grant was confirmed by Alexander III. in 1282, and by David II. in 1345, and again in 1364, Claypotts being then conjoined with "Craigy of Milton" and Balmaw.

The ground remained under the control of Lindores Abbey till the Reformation. Before that event the tenant who rented the lands from the Abbot in 1512 was John Strachan, who belonged to the family of Strachan of Carmyllie. His brother Gilbert was Canon of Brechin Cathedral, and founded a chaplaincy there. John Strachan of Claypotts (son of the preceding John) was in possession of the estate in 1556, and he and his son Gilbert were the builders of Claypotts Castle.

The dates at which different parts of the structure were erected are shown by the sculptured figures on two of the skew-stones, one of which bears the date "1569," and the other "1588," while a shield with the arms of Strachan and the initials "I.S." proves that John Strachan was the builder of the greater portion of the Castle. John Strachan was still living in 1584 at an advanced age, so that Gilbert would have little to do in completing the Castle.

It was in 1584 that Gilbert Strachan, then "younger of Claypotts," wedded Elizabeth, daughter of Alexander Maxwell of Tealing, and brought her to live at the Castle. He did not long survive his marriage, and he left an infant son as his heir. In those days it was reckoned an important office to have the guardianship of an heir during his minority; and apparently some of the Strachans had claimed "the right of wardship."

The widowed Lady of Claypotts seems to have been a strong-minded person; and she was backed by her four brothers, the Maxwells of Tealing. In 1593 they made up a plot to seize upon the Castle and carry off the heir. Coming to Claypotts with an armed band of their tenants, the Maxwells captured the fortalice and took possession of it; but the Strachans had expected this raid, and had sent off the child to Carmyllie for safety.

The Maxwells settled down at Claypotts, and this unnatural mother expected to enjoy the property during her life-time; but the Strachans brought a complaint against her before the Privy Council, and she was summarily ejected from the Castle. No record has been found of her later career.

Claypotts seemed destined to prove a bone of contention in the matrimonial affairs of the Strachans. When John Strachan had reached the age of 15 years he was served heir to his father, Gilbert Strachan. Three years afterwards— 1602—this precocious youth had the hardihood to marry a widow—Agnes Erskine, relict of Alexander Halkerton, who was probably much his senior in years. This marriage did not please the Halkertons, relatives of her deceased husband, and they so ridiculed and pestered her " at kirk and market " that her life was made miserable. She even began to dread that they would muster in force and attack her in "the tour and fortalice of Claypottis," so, for her own defence, she appealed for protection to the Privy Council.

An Order was issued commanding the Halkertons to cease from their persecution under heavy penalties. John Strachan did not long survive his marriage, and as he died without issue, he was the last of the Strachans of Claypotts. The superiority of the lands passed into the possession of John

Scrymgeoure, first Viscount Dudhope, who gave a charter of Claypotts to Sir William Graham of Claverhouse in 1625. Sir William before his death was proprietor of his ancestral home of Claverhouse; of the mansion of Glen Ogilvie, and of the Castle of Claypotts.

The Grahams of Claverhouse continued to hold Claypotts till the third generation. In 1672 the famous John Graham of Claverhouse was put in possession of it, and though his chief residence was Glen Ogilvie, he resided occasionally at Claypotts. At least, the consistent tradition in the locality associates his name with some of the ghostly tales told about the Castle.

As every reader of history knows, John Graham attained unenviable notoriety by his stern dealings with the Covenanters. No doubt the stories about his cruelty towards "the hill-folk" are greatly exaggerated; but even to this day he is remembered as much by the nickname of "Bluidy Claverse" as by the more complimentary designation of "Bonnie Dundee." There were current in the district early last century fearsome stories of wild orgies held by Claverhouse in the Castle of Claypotts —of mysterious convocations of witches, warlocks, and demons in this old building, over which the Laird of Claypotts presided as host, and at which he obtained from "Auld Hornie himsel'" that mystic power which made him safe from leaden bullets in the midst of the battle.

Under what conditions he made the bargain with the Devil is not known, nor whether he bartered his soul for wealth to satisfy his land-greed, and honours to ennoble him. But it is certain that the Covenanters believed that his fiery black charger was an animal of supernatural breed, and that the rider was bullet-proof through necromancy. Hence arose the story that on the field of Killiecrankie the hero fell, pierced to the heart not by a leaden bullet but by a silver button from the uniform of one of the opposing army. This superstition regarding Claverhouse survived till quite a recent date.

Not a hundred years ago it was confidently stated that on Hallowe'en—the night when witches in Scotland hold high revelry—the Castle of Claypotts has been seen by belated travellers lighted up with baleful fires; and sounds of wild delirium and eldricht sights have been heard and witnessed, such as recall the eerie cantrips at Alloway Kirk as detailed in "Tam o' Shanter."

It is useless to confute the legend of the orgies at Claypotts in the time of Claverhouse by declaring that he was a temperate man, too sensible to credit the foolish tales of witchcraft current in his time, and too upright to make any soul-destroying compact with the Devil. It is equally futile to suggest that the late wanderer in the vicinity on Hallowe'en who saw flashing lights in the Castle and heard weird sounds proceeding therefrom had probably been too long "boozin' at the nappie, and gettin' fou and unco happy," until he had reached an "elevated" condition. The notion that a "Witches' Sabbath" is still observed on Hallowe'en at Claypotts, in the presence of the Arch-Persecutor Claverhouse, has obtained too firm a hold to be deposed by common-sense argument.

This is not the only ghost-story connected with Claypotts. It has been averred that as the evening of 29th May in each year comes round there is visible at one of the upper windows of the Castle the figure of a White Lady, evidently in deep distress, waving a white handkerchief as a signal, and ever and anon wringing her hands in despair, as though her efforts to warn some loved one had been in vain.

Who is this mysterious lady that thus haunts the scenes of former pleasures, and views them only through a veil of tears? The popular explanation, which has long been traditional in the neighbourhood, is that she is Marion Ogilvy, daughter of the first Lord Airlie, who was the sweetheart of Cardinal Beaton—if indeed, she was not his wedded wife before he took priestly orders.

The story was that Cardinal Beaton built Claypotts for his beloved, and that from the upper window she could signal across the Tay to St. Andrews Bay, to warn her priestly lover that she was longing for his return. And on the 29th of May, 1546, she had waved her spotless kerchief in vain from the window of Claypotts, for her lover was then lying stark, cold, and still in the courtyard of St. Andrews Castle, ruthlessly slain by some of those who had been his dearest friends, the victim of a frantic outburst of ill-regulated religious fanaticism! And thus every year, as the fatal anniversary returns, the White Lady of Claypotts endures her weary vigil at the window of Claypotts Castle, and wails out her grief to the heedless wind.

It is useless to assert that David Beaton never had anything to do with Claypotts; that the dwelling-place of Marion Ogilvie was Melgund Castle, far out of range of St. Andrews; and that from the Ancient Cathedral City it would be quite impossible to see a 'kerchief waved from Claypotts. Nor will it even convert the believer in the tale to be told that nearly a quarter of a century had elapsed after the assassination of the Cardinal ere the present Castle was erected. This is one of the legends which is so firmly fixed that it is beyond the power of reason and common-sense to overturn.

Why should the ghosts of persons who actually joyed and sorrowed within these walls not haunt their beloved chambers, or wail through this desolate abode? Where is old John Strachan, the builder of the place which passed from his family in the third generation? Why does Elizabeth Maxwell, the widow of Gilbert Strachan, not utilise her power of tormenting the living, which her death must have vastly increased? And why does Viscount Dundee, instead of leading a rabble of rascal warlocks and randy witches, not return hither calm and dignified, with the glamour of victory on his brow, as he appeared when his faithful and sorrowing clansmen bore him wounded from the field of battle, to protest against the slanders and calumnies that have been ruthlessly cast upon his fair fame?

There is no more historical name associated with Claypotts than that of John Graham of Claverhouse; and here there is no deception. Many a time must he have looked out from these windows upon the broadly sweeping course of the Tay. Within these deserted chambers he must often have pondered his ambitious schemes, or planned his valiant enterprises. Fascinating as are the weird ghost-stories of Claypotts Castle, the true incidents connected with this venerable structure are not less captivating.

Ringing, piping and bawling out the news

THE death in December, 1904, of Charles Harris, the Dundee Bellman, naturally recalled the memory of some of his predecessors in that once important office. Several of the Bellmen of other days were eccentric characters, and their official duties frequently afforded opportunities for the display of native humour. Two public functionaries, the Town Drummer and the Town Crier or Bellman, long existed contemporaneously; but the former office was abolished in 1833, when Dan M'Cormick, "the learned Town Drummer of Dundee," expired.

In early times—as far back, indeed, as the existing Town Records, that is, from about 1550—the Town Drummer's duty was to make all proclamations, national, civic, and social, in the burgh. Thus, when the Lockit-Book was to be opened for the enrolment of burgesses, the Town Drummer was sent through the burgh to warn the inhabitants "by touk of drum" that this solemn ceremony was about to be performed. It was also the task of the Town Drummer to summon the burghers to arms when an enemy was expected, and to rouse the warlike ardour of the Dundonians by his martial music.

The Town Bellman, though also a civic official, was at the service of the inhabitants for the purpose of making personal announcements. From an entry in the Town Council minutes for 1556 it appears that the Bellman was "to tak na mair for his ance passing throw the toun at the desyre of ony neighbour nor twa pennies." His office at that time was often conjoined with that of Sexton; and in 1556 it was distinctly laid down by the Town Council that his fees for "making of graves" in St. Clement's Churchyard (now the Vault), then the place of interment, should be—"for ane man's grave, twelf pennies, and for ane bairn's grave, ane plack, and for puir creatures that hes na thing—na thing."

After the Reformation another official was appointed as "Piper of Dundee," his duty being to march through the burgh, "dressed in the town's livery and colours," playing on his bagpipes, every morning at four o'clock, to arouse the workmen to the labours of the day, and every evening at eight o'clock to warn them to seek their rest. This plan was adopted as a substitute for the matin-bell and curfew of pre-Reformation times; but the Piper vanished from the streets of Dundee centuries ago. Thus the Piper and the Drummer have both disappeared, and the Town Bellman alone has survived to our own day.

During the early half of last century there were four successive Bellmen in Dundee, each being a character in his way. The first of these was James Paterson, who was appointed to the post in 1819, and continued in the practice of his "calling" for over 16 years. He was a native of Dundee, and was bred to the sea, serving for a long time on the whalers that then made Dundee a very prosperous port.

A curious custom then existed. As in those days there was no telegraph to send word home of the success of a whaler as soon as she had touched at a northern port, the condition of the vessel was not made known until she reached the Firth of Tay. The method of conveying early information was for the whaler, whenever she entered the Tay, to fire from her guns a number of shots equal to the number of fish captured. While the North Sea was still in an unsettled state during the Napoleonic Wars, the whalers had to carry large carronades for their own protection; and the booming of these heavy guns was heard across a long distance.

On one occasion, when James Paterson was loading a signal-gun, the charge exploded, depriving him of his left hand. This was a serious matter for him, because he was "caury-fisted" (that is, left-handed), and he was even more helpless than a normal seaman would have been with his right hand uninjured. Having been thus forced to abandon seafaring life, Paterson settled on shore, taking a small public-house in Fish Street, the spot most frequented by seamen.

But, alas! James Paterson became "ane o' his ain best customers," and his frank manners and jovial disposition brought him to ruin. Just when this misfortune had overtaken him, the post of Bellman and Town Crier became vacant; and as Paterson was then in very straitened circumstances, his appointment was an act of charity. He soon became a local character, familiarly known to all the inhabitants as "Jamie Paiterson."

From passing allusions in the "Dundee Advertiser" during the time of Paterson's service, a fair idea may be formed of his appearance and manner. His voice was full and sonorous, as befitted one who had "out-blustered Boreas" in the Arctic regions; though sometimes, when he had imbibed "potations, pottle-deep," his articulation became somewhat mixed. It is recorded that "at times it was amusing to hear him as he proceeded on his rounds, proclaiming sales of merchandise, the loss or recovery of money, the straying or finding of children, or the arrival of fishermen with extra catches of haddocks, his proclamations being uttered in Doric style with pertinent comments of his own."

An odd instance of his extreme candour is thus narrated:—
"If he had to announce the loss of bank notes, or any article of value, he would add that the numbers of the notes were known, or that the loser was in possession of such information

as would prevent any one from appropriating the missing property. But no sooner was the proclamation made than he would address such of his acquaintances as he might perceive among the listeners in these terms:—" 'Deed, we ken naething aboot the nummers o' the notes; that's jeest said to gar them that hae them gie them up." Paterson died suddenly on 11th February, 1836, and gave place to the more notable Bellman.

The new Town Crier and Bellman was selected, according to the Town Council Minutes, "from a large number of applicants;" and though Joseph Dempster held the office for little more than four years, he was long remembered in Dundee. Dempster was a boot and shoemaker in Edinburgh for a number of years, and had formed a good business, but misfortune overtook him, and he left the Scottish Metropolis to settle in Dundee. Here he struggled for some time to form a connection, but with little success. His capital was small, and the custom of the period demanded long credit, which Dempster was not in a position to give.

An anonymous correspondent, writing to the "Dundee Advertiser" of 7th August, 1840 (after Dempster's death), gives some stories regarding "Josie" while he was a bootmaker and a member of the Cordiner Craft. Despite his adversities, Dempster never lost heart, and could joke at his misfortunes even when they seemed hardest. He had fed and nourished a porker, intending it for the support of his young family; but the animal was poinded by a messenger-at-arms for debt. "Fare ye weel, Sandy Cawmel," was his parting salutation to the pig, "ye'll no hae lang noo to mind yer auld maister. The Lord giveth, and the Lord taketh away— Blessed be His holy name!"

Referring to an old shopmate, Dempster once said:— "M—— is a man of original genius, and of great invention. I aince thocht I was his equal. I could work as well as he, and even yet I could eat wi' him, drink wi' him, sing wi' him, or pray wi' him; but for tellin' lies he was a cut abune me— I never could touch him at that."

Once Dempster took a pair of boots to Dudhope Castle for one of the officers of the regiment quartered there, expecting the money to be paid on delivery. He overheard the officers order his servant to tell the fellow to call back, as he was not in. Joseph immediately popped in his bald head, with the query, "Pray, sir, when will your honour be in?"

Though Joseph could look sharply after what was due to him at times, he never could succeed in accumulating money, and was frequently put to sad shifts for the needful. Having once an order for a pair of shoes, he found it extremely difficult to get the necessary materials for them. He had leather for the soles, but not for the uppers, and he was nearly at his wits' end as to how he was to get it. Joseph was fertile in expedients. Having a quarto Bible bound in calf, he took the leather from it, blackened it over, made the uppers with it, and thus completed the job.

His trade of shoemaker supplied him once with an apt comparison. Some one in his hearing remarked about an untoward occurrence that "such was the will of Providence." Joseph observed that the word "Providence" was a very handy one—it was a sort of japan blacking to give a smooth skin to what otherwise would not bear inspection. In his early days, when serving as a shopman, Dempster had been charged by his clergyman with "making lies," an accusation sometimes brought against his craft. "No, no," replied Joseph, indignantly, "my master makes the lies; I only retail them."

The appointment of Dempster to the post of Bellman was an act of municipal kindness, as in 1836 he was in extreme distress; but he amply justified his selection. Many stories are told about the droll humour displayed in the exercise of his vocation. The "Dundee Advertiser" of 24th August, 1838, contains the following paragraph:—"The Bellman at the close of last week announced a serious loss which had befallen a householder in Fish Street. It was nothing less than the loss of his wife and child. 'Lost!' said the eccentric Bellman, 'belonging to a man, his wife, and a child along with her. Whoever can give such information as may lead to the recovery of the child will be handsomely rewarded; but,' continued the Bellman, with a swing round and great emphasis, 'the wife is not wanted.'"

On another occasion Dempster made the following intimation:—"Lost, between the top of the Murraygate and the Wellgate, five five-pound notes. Whoever will return the same will be handsomely rewarded.—I dinna believe it; they were lost some ither gait!"

A curious story is told as to how Dempster once magnified his office. Sir John Monro was in command of a detachment of the 71st Highland Regiment, quartered in Dudhope Castle, and he had the misfortune to lose his dog. The Bellman was engaged to make proclamation of the loss, but he had some difficulty in obtaining payment of his fee. One day, however, he donned his "berrial blacks" and went up to the Barracks. He found that Sir John was there, and he directed the orderly to inform him that "one of the officials of Dundee wishes to see him." This message brought out Sir John, who inquired curtly, "Who are you, sir?"

With an obsequious bow, Joseph answered—"You are the Right Honourable Sir John Monro, and I am the Honourable the Bellman of Dundee."

The purpose of the visit was disclosed, and Dempster obtained the half-crown that was due to him, when, making a profound obeisance, the Bellman said—"I thank the Most Honourable Sir John Munro for his patronage and generosity."

Joseph Dempster was a member of the Seceders' Kirk, and for several years was precentor there. This brought him into good-humoured discussions with the clergy of the Auld Kirk, and his native wit often brought him off victorious. One day the Rev. George Tod, of St. David's Church, was chaffing Joseph, and he smartly took him up thus:—"Ou ay; I've heard you preachin' aboot Balaam's ass; but I'll wager, wi' a' yer Bible knowledge, ye couldna tell me what Awbraham's coo said whan he gied her a poke wi' his staff." "No, I could not, Joseph," said Mr. Tod, "and I don't think you could tell either, if it had to be told." "Hoot awa', man," said Joseph, "it jist cried ' Boo,' like ony ither coo!"

One day Joseph sprained his ankle on the High Street, and Dr. Crichton, who happened to pass, was asked for his advice. Being himself a humorist, the doctor thought to frighten Dempster. Shaking his head seriously, he said he was afraid the leg would have to be taken off. "Weel, weel," said Joseph contentedly, "in that case I'll rin the lichter."

Dempster lived in the Thorter Row, and on the evening of Tuesday, 28th July, 1840, he was coming down the stair leading from his house when his foot slipped, and he fell to the bottom, landing on his head. He was taken up, and medical aid procured, but at four o'clock on the following morning he passed away.

The newspapers of the time bore testimony to the esteem with which he was regarded. One writer says:—"However trifling the matter Joseph had to publish, his manner of doing it always attracted the attention of the passers-by. No Sovereign in Europe could address his Parliament or Diet with more pomposity than he announced the sale of a quantity of furniture in the Greenmarket, or the sailing of a steam vessel. In private life Joseph was highly esteemed for his general kindness and urbanity of manners. As far as his limited means would allow, he was always ready to assist the needy and destitute." No better epitaph need be desired than this, so frankly pronounced over Josie Dempster.

On 21st August, 1840, the Town Council appointed Alexander Ferguson to the post of Bellman, vacant by Dempster's death. He did not long enjoy the honours and emoluments, as he died in January, 1843, and has left no special record.

In the following month he was succeeded by another of the same name, and the fact of two Alexander Fergusons being in office successively has led to some confusion. The second Sandy Ferguson continued to perform his duties as Bellman till 22nd February, 1849, having thus completed six years of service.

There was a very odd circumstance connected with the second Alexander Ferguson. Shortly after his appointment as Bellman he fell on the ice and became cripple. From that time forth he had to obtain the aid of a donkey to assist in his official work, and there was something ludicrous in the appearance of Sandy Ferguson, mounted like Balaam on an ass, and solemnly ringing his bell to make proclamations. Ferguson, it is said, was a simple and inoffensive man, and although not distinguished for wit or personal eccentricity, his advent to the Greenmarket or High Street upon his Rosinante was sure to gather a crowd around him. His successor was Alexander Young, flax-dresser, who was appointed Bellman on 7th April, 1849, and regarding whom history is silent.

By the middle of last century the newspapers had gained such a hold upon the people that an advertisement was of far more value than the announcements of the Bellman, which could only reach a few of the inhabitants. The office gradually became little more than a sinecure—a relic of times that had wholly passed away.

Wonderful story of Dan the Drummer man

THERE have long been current in this quarter several floating traditions about Dan M'Cormick, the Town Drummer of Dundee, some of the stories being true, and others evidently invented. But the true story of Dan M'Cormick is even more wonderful than any of the fables that have been concocted regarding him. More than ninety years have elapsed since his death, and there can be no one alive who can remember Dan's appearance. Yet his name has been so long familiar to Dundonians that an outline of his career will be interesting to many readers.

Though Dan M'Cormick was a prominent official in Dundee for over 30 years, there was little known during his life-time of the strange events in his career before he came to the burgh. His parents belonged to Lochaber, his father being in business as a dyer, apparently at Fort-William. He had succeeded in making a fair living there, but being ambitious and desirous of a larger field for the exercise of his abilities, he removed to London about 1758, and pursued his trade there. Much mystery surrounds this incident, and Dan M'Cormick was very reticent regarding it.

The likeliest theory is that Dan's father was "out in the '45," as there were six M'Cormicks from Fort William among the followers of Stewart of Appin, on the side of Prince Charlie, five of whom were slain at Culloden, and one escaped with a wound. It seems very probable that the father of Dan was this hero; that he returned to his old occupation; but that the strong feeling against the Stewart vassals which arose about the time of the execution of James Stewart of Acharn for the alleged murder of Colin Campbell of Glenure made it expedient for M'Cormick to "gang south." At least, it is certain that he settled in the east end of London; and there his son Dan was born about 1760.

Misfortune overtook the M'Cormick family. The father was not successful in business. The mother died, leaving an only son; and while Dan was a mere lad the death of his father left him a penniless orphan. Dan had been employed in his father's trade, but he was too young to battle alone in a strange land. Some of his kinsfolk in Lochaber persuaded him to return to the home of his fathers, and about 1775 he left London for Fort-William.

He had no trade save that of his father, and he tried to re-establish the old connection which the elder M'Cormick had formed. The attempt was unsuccessful, and, indeed, he was not fitted to conduct a business with small capital. His tastes were literary, not commercial, and when he was reduced to straits he determined to wind up his affairs and to leave Lochaber, to which place he was to return no more.

It was about 1780 that Dan M'Cormick made his way to Glasgow, his poverty drawing him thither that he might earn his daily bread, whilst his thirst for book-knowledge made him prefer a University town which had also a large commercial population. What occupation he followed in Glasgow is not known, though it is likely that he would find employment at some of the mills where dyeing work was carried on. In his leisure hours he assiduously devoted himself to study, and as "a lad o' pairts" he made considerable progress in his self-education.

Meanwhile his clansmen in Lochaber, having heard of Dan's devotion to literature, took steps to have him educated for the Roman Catholic priesthood. He had displayed an astonishing faculty for acquiring languages; and it might have been possible to have gained admission for him as a student of the Scots College in Paris, or at one of the establishments for Scotch students in Rome and in Valladolid. Here the element of mystery comes again into Dan M'Cormick's life. He did not enter any of these Colleges, and if the case was adopted by any of the few wealthy Roman Catholics then in Glasgow, no record has been preserved of the steps taken.

Nevertheless, the fact is unimpeachable that he became a miniature Mezzofanti in his mastery of languages; and in his early days knew Hebrew, Greek, and Latin, besides his Gaelic mother tongue, so that he must have had some tutor able to instruct him orally, for the means of self-instruction in those days were very meagre.

What was it that interrupted a career of so much promise, and imposed a barrier to his progress which he was never able to surmount ? What hindered Dan M'Cormick from becoming the most learned priest in Scotland instead of a mere civic official with limited and formal duties ? That will never be known. It was while Dan lived in Glasgow that fierce anti-Popish riots raged, and all the Roman Catholics—then but a small number—were put under the ban.

He may have wavered in his attachment to the creed of his fathers; or, more probably a love affair taught him that he was not well-fitted to become a celibate priest. Whatever was the obscure cause, he definitely abandoned his purpose, and about 1790 he enlisted in the 5th or Argyllshire Regiment of Fencibles, resigning the gown of the priest that he might take up the sword of the soldier.

For nine years Dan M'Cormick served in the ranks as a common soldier. His learning did not enable him to attain a higher grade, though his conduct must have been irreproachable from the following incident in his career. The Argyllshire Fencibles, under Lieutenant-Colonel J. Campbell, were quartered at Dudhope Castle—then used regularly as the Barracks—from October 6, 1798, till March 11, 1799, and during that time Dan M'Cormick had come into contact with the famous Provost Riddoch. The dread of a French Invasion was then prevalent, and the Provost, being of a martial disposition, set about raising a Forfarshire Regiment of Volunteers.

On 11th March, 1797, the Town Council offered to raise a body of men, to be called the Second or Light Infantry Dundee Volunteers, reserving the post of Colonel for the Provost ex-officio, and nominating officers. The Government accepted the offer, and the corps was ultimately formed by Provost Riddoch.

To assist him in organizing this Regiment he procured, through personal influence, the discharge of Dan M'Cormick and some of his comrades; and these were installed as the Drill Instructors of the first Dundee Volunteers. Dan's ability placed him in a rank superior to that of his comrades; and to make sure that he would not leave the burgh he was appointed by special Act of Council, dated 9th November, 1801, one of the Town's Officers, and was thus thirled to Dundee.

So rapidly did M'Cormick fulfil his task that in February, 1804, the 4th Battalion of the Forfarshire Volunteers, numbering 357 officers and men, was quartered in Dudhope Castle, and remained in barracks for over two months. The officers were Lieutenant-Colonel Riddoch and Major William Scott. During April, 1804, the 1st Battalion of the Forfarshire Volunteers (300 men) under Lieutenant-Colonel John Colvill, did barrack duty for a month at Dudhope Castle, so Dan M'Cormick was kept fully employed.

The accidental circumstance of M'Cormick being in Dundee as a common soldier had thus the effect of settling the rest of his career. In 1810 he was appointed Town Drummer, his duty being to make proclamations by tuck of drum, and to perform the civic and official duties which did not fall within the province of the Bellman. Dan had spent his leisure hours as a soldier in extending his linguistic studies.

He had mastered several tongues which now only fall under the cognizance of a Professor of Oriental Languages. Gaelic he had known from infancy; Hebrew, Greek, and Latin he had acquired in Glasgow; Welsh he had studied in Jones and Morris's Dictionary and Grammar; he had wrestled with Arabic, struggled with Syriac, had more than a bowing acquaintance with Samaritan, and was familiar with the current literature of France, Germany, and Italy. Indeed, had he been Town Drummer of some cosmopolitan port in the Mediterranean, he might have made his announcements in about twelve different languages.

Besides all these accomplishments, it is recorded by a contemporary that "he was well skilled in music, and while in the vigour of life his performance on wind-instruments was considered excellent." Truly, one might have searched the kingdom through without finding so rare a phenomenon as the learned Town Drummer of Dundee.

While thus going on his official rounds as Drummer, and acting as Town Officer and Billet-Master—for Dan was a pluralist—M'Cormick still kept up his literary studies. He had gathered together many special works relating to the languages with which he was familiar, and the mania for book-collecting took hold upon him after his settlement in Dundee. He had then means for accommodating books such as he could not have in barracks as a soldier; and in course of time he collected a very remarkable library. Its extent and quality may be imagined when it is stated that the sale of M'Cormick's books after his death was spread over five days.

The catalogue of this sale, which took place in the rooms of John Carfrae & Son, Edinburgh, from 1st to 5th April, 1833, shows 795 lots, including considerably over 1000 volumes. There were books on Divinity, Oriental and Biblical Literature, Philology, Classics, and general literature in Greek, Latin, Hebrew, Gaelic, French, and German. Many of the volumes were of the sixteenth and seventeenth centuries, and would bring large prices at the present day. Modern literature was represented by first editions of most of Scott's novels and poems; Byron's works, volumes by Mrs. Hemans, Barry Cornwall, Jane Porter, Maria Edgeworth, and Burns. Hebrew seems to have been M'Cormick's favourite study, as he had quite a number of rare publications in that language. And thereby hangs a tale.

It is related that on one occasion a Professor of Hebrew visited Dundee for the purpose of forming classes for the teaching of that language. He interviewed one of the ministers in the town, and while they were walking along the High Street they encountered Dan M'Cormick. The cleric, being a wag, thought he would have a joke at the expense of the Professor, and, stopping Dan, he introduced him to the stranger as the Town Drummer, and explained the cause of the Professor's visit. Dan began to question him as to his method of teaching Hebrew, and pulled a Hebrew Psalter out of his pocket to illustrate his remarks. The Professor stood aghast! Evidently there was no room for him in a burgh where the Town Drummer knew more about Hebrew than he did; so he quietly decamped.

Another version of this story was long current. A Professor of Hebrew did visit the town for the purpose stated, and called upon a venerable D.D. to ask his advice. The Doctor referred him to Dan M'Cormick, and the Professor, having found Dan, had a long and delighted conversation with him on many recondite subjects. His conclusion, freely expressed afterwards, was that the Town Drummer would have made an excellent Doctor of Divinity, while the Doctor of Divinity was only fit to be a Town Drummer!

Whether M'Cormick had been disappointed in love early

in life, or had merely thought that marriage would distract him from his studies, is not known. He was never married, though, as a writer remarked at the time of his death, "he lived the life of a bachelor, but he was not indifferent to the attractions of the fair. He has left a daughter behind him." It is not improbable that an attachment formed by him while in Glasgow was rudely broken off for some obscure reason, and thus the whole current of his life was altered. Where the daughter came from, or where she disappeared, is not recorded. Dan M'Cormick died on 14th December, 1832, having been in the service of the town for over 30 years.

No sooner was the death of Dan M'Cormick, the Town Drummer, announced, than applications for the office poured in to the Town Clerk. From the Council minutes of 27th December, 1832, it appears that no fewer than ten aspirants had sent in petitions. Among these were two sergeants of police, a vintner, a spirit-dealer, and two sheriff officers, and, strangely enough, Arthur Wood, auctioneer, who was executed for murder in 1838, was ambitious to serve the burgh as Town Drummer.

The Magistrates were directed to consider the expediency of separating the three offices which M'Cormick filled as Drummer, Town's Officer, and Billet Master. The Magistrates reported to the Town Council on 31st January, 1833, and the matter appears thus in the minutes:—

"The Council on considering a report from the Magistrates on the remit to them contained in the Council minutes of 27th December last, resolved that it is inexpedient to supply the vacancy occasioned by the death of the late Daniel M'Cormick, Town Officer and Town Drummer, by the appointment of an officer with the usual salary. The Council, therefore, in terms of the recommendation of the Magistrates, nominated and appointed, and do hereby, with the declaration after-mentioned, nominate and appoint John Fraser, sheriff officer in Dundee, to be a Town Officer and Town Drummer in the burgh of Dundee, as enlarged, during the pleasure of the Council; under which appointment it is specially declared that the said John Fraser shall only be entitled to receive the usual suit of clothes yearly; but he shall not be entitled to any salary or other emolument from the Council; his emoluments under the appointment being limited to his Officer's dues for the execution of Burgh Court Summons, Decrees, Precepts, and other writs; and to the usual allowance as Town Drummer for proclaiming notices, proclamations, and advertisements by the Drum; and these emoluments, dues, or allowances to be payable by his employers in these capacities."

James Miln, Council Officer, was appointed Billet Master at a yearly salary of five pounds.

John Fraser continued in office as Town Drummer for a long period. He was succeeded by James Baird, who acted in that capacity from about 1851 till 1871. His assistant, Graham Laing, became official Town Drummer at that date, and continued till 1878. James Robertson, Council Officer, was then appointed, and the triple offices were renewed; but he only acted officially once as Drummer, proclaiming the Lady Fair in 1878. He acted as Billet-Master up till 13th December 1880, but this office was then transferred by Act of Parliament to the Chief Constable. James Robertson died in November, 1911, having filled the office for 34 years. The Council officers are now the sole representatives of the former civic dignity of Dundee.

From ale-sellers to soul savers — family Lamb's great crusade

THE death of Mr. James W. Lamb, of Lamb's Hotel, which took place on December 31, 1904, removed the last of the sons of Thomas Lamb, whose name was long familiar in Dundee. It may interest readers to know the veritable history of a family that for many years exercised a powerful moral influence in the city.

Even though the designation of "Lamb's Hotel" has now disappeared, the name will be preserved by the magnificent Lamb Collection of local history and antiquities, now located in the Dundee Museum; and future generations will more fully appreciate the work accomplished by the members of this family than their contemporaries have done. Nearly a century and a quarter has elapsed since Thomas Lamb was born, and during the first half of last century he was privileged to do more practical good in reforming social customs than almost any other citizen of Dundee.

Thomas Lamb was born in 1801, within the house in Lamb's Lane, Forebank, Dundee—a narrow thoroughfare that runs parallel with Dens Road—which was occupied by his father, John Lamb, manufacturer. The name of Lamb's Lane had been given to this street because at an earlier time it had led to the humble "four-loom shop" of John Lamb's elder brother; and even so far down in time as 1822, the name of this John Lamb figures as a manufacturer "in the Dens."

So far as the family tradition goes, John Lamb was a stern Calvinist and a thoroughly upright man—one of the old type of Scotsmen who preserved a savour of Covenanting times even amid modern development.

As a boy, Thomas Lamb was strictly trained in the tenets of the older school of theology, his practical education being obtained in the nearest parochial school. Brief time was then allowed for scholastic training, and young Lamb was soon put to learn handloom-weaving, which was then the most lucrative employment.

His mind, however, did not lie towards a mechanical craft. He had often wandered out to the Den of the Mains, to Baldovan, and to the Sidlaws, and studied natural botany in scenes of "Nature's wildest grandeur." So ardent did his love of nature become that he gave up the loom for the spade, and served his apprenticeship as a gardener with a nurseryman in Cupar-Fife. He obtained a situation as gardener at Castle Huntly, in the Carse of Gowrie, and remained there several years, till his health broke down, and he was compelled to resign.

Being both frugal and industrious, Thomas Lamb had saved some money, and he was advised to use his capital to start as a grocer, and afterwards as a spirit dealer. He rented a shop at the east end of the Murraygate, and carried on for some time a fairly successful business.

After two years of this occupation, in 1828 he married Miss Crawford, daughter of Alexander Crawford, shoemaker, a member of a family that had long been connected with the Cordiner Craft in Dundee. Miss Crawford was then scarcely out of her teens, having been born in her father's house at Fairmuir in 1808; but she was of a practical turn of mind, and proved a faithful and industrious wife.

Shortly after this marriage there began in Dundee the first Temperance Crusade, and Mr. Lamb attended, through curiosity, some of the meetings, and heard especially the stirring addresses delivered by William Cruickshanks, known as "the teetotal coal-carter." He was deeply impressed by the descriptions of the horrors caused by excessive drinking, and he determined that he would no longer have a share in causing such ruin and misery. He discussed the matter with his wife, who entirely agreed with him; and they decided to give up the spirit trade.

A mere business man would have striven to regain his ill-invested capital by selling the drink he had purchased; but Thomas Lamb was too sincere and straightforward to take this method. He had only had the license for a few months when he and his wife, with their own hands, emptied all the alcoholic liquor in their possession into the drain. This apparently Quixotic proceeding almost spelled ruin for them at first; though ultimately it brought them many friends. Mr. James Brown of Lochton, and others who had adopted the temperance principles, rallied to the support of the Lambs.

Often in later years, Mrs. Lamb declared that the happiest moment of her life was when she got rid of "the accursed thing," which weighed like an incubus upon them both. Nevertheless, they had practically to begin life again.

Thomas Lamb's practical mind early discovered that if young men were to be kept secure from the temptations of the public-house, some other attractions must be offered. Accordingly he removed in 1830 to the premises at 30 Murraygate, on the south side of the street, and conducted his grocer's business in the shop, fitting up the flat above as a coffee-room, supplied with newspapers. The plan succeeded beyond anticipation. In 1833 he added the manufacture of pastry and confectionery to his other business, and soon became one of the best purveyors in town.

The Coffee-Room in the Murraygate was speedily one of the literary centres in Dundee. The Literary Societies, which had formerly met in various small and cheerless rooms in different parts of the town, now found it more convenient to hold their meetings in Mr. Lamb's comfortable establishment. In all these meetings Mr. Lamb took a kindly and paternal interest.

The first of these Societies to make the Dundee Coffee-House a regular resort was "The Literary Coterie," afterwards named "The Dundee Literary Institute;" and with it were connected some of the young men of about a hundred years ago, not a few of whom attained to literary fame. The "Dundee Naturalists' Association," led by George Lawson, afterwards Professor Lawson of Canada; the "Literary and Scientific Institute," with James Adie, the geologist, at its head; the "Literary Emporium," with which the late Rev. James Inches Hillocks was connected; and the "Dundee Temperance Mutual Improvement Society," were all wont to hold their meetings in the famous Murraygate establishment.

The name of "The Halls of Lamb" was given to the place in consequence of a parody on Byron's "Isles of Greece," which was written by Mr. John Syme, and in which the poet seemed to return to the scene of former literary contests:—

The Halls of Lamb! the Halls of Lamb!
Where Scrymgeour fought and Henry sung,
Where on the lips of Tawse and Cramb
"The Union" once enchanted hung—
The Old Gas Company lights them yet,
But all their ancient glory's set.

The late Mr. John Paul in his Inaugural Address as President of the Dundee Burns Society, on October, 1904, took "The Halls of Lamb" as his subject, and identified all the heroes named in the poem.

The Murraygate business became so prosperous that the place had to be extended; but in 1838 Mr. Lamb put into practice a new idea. At that time only about one half of Reform Street had been built, the portion furthest from the High Street being then a receptacle for refuse of all kinds.

Mr. Lamb leased a part of this ground, at the corner of the Howff, from the Hospital, and there he erected a wooden building—on the site of the later hotel—which he called the "Tea Gardens." His advertisement, which appeared in the "Dundee Advertiser" of 13th July, 1838, sufficiently describes the place:—

> Thomas Lamb, confectioner, Murraygate, respectfully solicits a visitation to the Saloon, top of Reform Street, west side, which he opened on the day of Her Majesty's Coronation, and which he is to continue during the summer months, for the sale of confectionery, ginger beer, tarts, pies, biscuits, etc. Newspapers taken in—Dundee Advertiser, Courier, and Chronicle; Edinburgh Scotsman, Pilot, and Scottish Guardian, Tait's Magazine, and Chambers's Journal.

This venture was so successful that in November, 1838, Mr. Lamb opened another saloon behind the first one, and occupied it as a Reading-Room and tea and coffee-house. In his advertisement of 2nd November, he states "it is opened on the principles of those who are opposed to the use of intoxicating liquors, alcohol not being among the articles sold."

The shop at 30 Murraygate was left in the charge of Mrs. Lamb, while her husband devoted much attention to the Reform Street Saloon.

The next development of the Saloon was the erection of a

Hall for meetings, capable of accommodating 200 people. In 1843 an additional piece of ground on the south of the saloon was rented, and here Mr Lamb used his skill as a gardener by laying it out with flower-beds, gravel walks, a rockery, fish pond, and fountain—quite a pleasure garden on a miniature scale. It was opened on 28th June, 1843, and soon became a popular resort.

In December of the following year Mr. Lamb opened another Coffee-House at the West Port, which Mrs. Lamb took under her charge, while the eldest daughter, Miss Lamb (Mrs. Kidd), looked after the Murraygate establishment. A great change was made shortly afterwards. Mr. Lamb believed that a temperance hotel for commercial travellers would prove as popular as the residential hotels that had been put up in Edinburgh and Glasgow. Accordingly he feued part of the Tea Gardens ground in Reform Street, and built the first part of the Hotel.

On 30th July, 1852, Lamb's Temperance Hotel was opened, Lord Kinnaird presiding at the ceremony. For 14 years the hotel progressed rapidly. At length, in March 1866, Mr. Lamb acquired the ground at the north-west corner of Reform Street, and built the handsome block that formed the Hotel, which was opened in the autumn of 1867, shortly before the meeting of the British Association in Dundee. The business was then concentrated in this one spot, the shops in Murraygate and West Port having been given up.

Having started the Hotel on the best lines then adopted by similar institutions in Edinburgh and Glasgow, Mr. Lamb next turned his attention to dairy-farming. He rented Brewhead Cottage, near Birkhill, and devised a model farm there. But fate had decreed that he was not to see the result of all his labours. In 1868 he fell into bad health, and on 31st October, 1869, he died, being then 68 years of age.

The hotel business was successfully carried on by Mrs. Lamb and her two sons, A. C. Lamb and J. W. Lamb, with Miss Eliza Lamb. All these have now passed away. Mrs. Lamb survived her husband for almost 20 years, dying on 21st March, 1889. Miss Lamb's death took place on 2nd July, 1894. Mr. A. C. Lamb died on 29th April, 1897; and Mr. J. W. Lamb on 31st December, 1904. Thus the story of Thomas Lamb and his family covers the whole of the nineteenth century.

After the death of Thomas Lamb, the most prominent member of the family was his elder son, Alexander Crawford Lamb, whose name for many years was a household word in Dundee. He was born on 21st February, 1843, and educated at the High School. Having the prospect of succeeding to the control of his father's business, he was regularly apprenticed to the baking trade, and afterwards held situations in hotels at Liverpool, Manchester, and Edinburgh. He was 26 years of age when he returned to Dundee to take the position vacant through his father's death; and from that time till his death in 1897 he was the principal active partner in the firm.

While immersed in business, Mr. Lamb found leisure to cultivate his literary and artistic tastes. He formed a very select cabinet of valuable pictures, and his library at the time of his death contained many rare works, among these being the "unique" copy of the first Kilmarnock edition of Burns's Poems, which was sold at the then extreme price of £572. But it was as a collector of relics of Dundee that Mr. Lamb did the greatest service to his native city.

When the Improvement Act of 1871 came into operation, Mr. A. C. Lamb foresaw that many of the old charactertistic buildings would be demolished. He began, therefore, to preserve records of these by photographs and drawings, and as he was constantly adding to this private local museum he had formed an extensive collection of maps, views, antiquities of various kinds, portraits of notable Dundonians, and relics of Dundee. In 1892-93, when the Old Dundee Exhibition was organised, a large proportion of the exhibits was from Mr. Lamb's collection. Some time after his death in 1897, it seemed likely that these treasures, which had taken about 30 years to bring together, would be dispersed; but in November, 1901, Mr. Edward Cox generously came forward, acquired the collection, and presented it to Dundee for preservation in the Museum. The Lamb Collection has no precise parallel in any of the Scottish cities; and it will long serve to perpetuate the memory of one of Dundee's most loyal citizens. The elaborate book which was brought out by Mr. Lamb under the title of "Dundee: Its Quaint and Historical Buildings," is equally without a rival in Scotland. Verily, the members of the Lamb family have accomplished much for their native city.

After the death of Mr. James Lamb in 1904, the business was transformed into "Lamb's Hotel Limited," and was managed by his surviving daughter, Miss Lamb, and his son-in-law, Mr. George Kerr. The Hotel had become such a favourite resort both for visitors and residents that it was a veritable landmark in the City. At length, in 1922, the Limited Liability Company was wound up, and the building was acquired and fitted up for business premises under the designation of "Meadow House." Portions of the original building are still occupied as Restaurants, but there is no longer a "Lamb's Hotel."

Drink emptied down the drain

Queen Mary summons her people to war

THE connection of Dundee with the Royal Family of Scotland dates from a very early period. There is a tradition that Malcolm Canmore, who reigned from 1057 till 1093, had a residence in the burgh, though proof of this statement has not been found. Malcolm's seventh son, Eadgar, began to reign in 1097, and it is stated that he died at Dundee in 1107.

Some of the old chroniclers record that Eadgar's death took place "in Dunedin," though Andrew Wyntoun, the Prior of Lochleven, who wrote his rhyming Chronicle about 1406, distinctly states the place of Eadgar's death to have been Dundee. As he uses the name as a rhyme-word, he could not mistake it, and though sometimes poets are driven to severe straits to get their rhymes to clink, it is not likely that Wyntoun would have introduced Dundee instead of Dunedin. He may have been misinformed, however. The passage in Wyntoun's quaint old Scottish language reads thus :—

> A thowsand a hundyre yhere and seven
> Fra Mary bare the Kyng off Hevyn,
> Off Edgare, oure nobill Kyng,
> The dayis wyth honoure tuk endyng;
> Be-north Tay in till Dunde
> Tyll God the spyryte than yhald he.
> And in the Kyrk off Dwnfermlyne
> Solemply he was enteryd syne.

If the alleged house of King Malcolm Canmore was in Dundee, it seems to have passed out of the possession of his successors, for when they visited Dundee, they either resided with the Constable at Dudhope Castle, in the Franciscan Monastery, or in the house in the Seagate which belonged to the Abbots of Balmerino. The exact dates when the early Scottish monarchs visited Dundee can be discovered by the charters and deeds which they signed here.

On 9th February, 1226-7, Alexander II. granted a charter to the Preaching Friars of St. Andrews, which he signed at Dundee. Alexander III. signed a charter to the Abbey of

Balmerino, dated at Dundee, 18th July, 1285. King John Balliol (whose mother, Devorgilla, founded the Franciscan Monastery) summoned certain of his subjects to do homage to him at Dundee on 24th February, 1292-3.
When Edward I. of England marched through Scotland, he arrived at Dundee on 6th August, 1296, and remained for one night, probably staying in the Castle. Robert the Bruce was twice in Dundee—on 21st October, 1314, a few months after Bannockburn, and again on 29th November, 1327, shortly after the death of his Queen. David II. was long a prisoner in England, yet he visited Dundee no less than eleven times between 1342 and 1370, and during the last five years of his life he paid the burgh an annual visit.

Robert II., the first of the Stewart Kings, was an almost annual visitor. His son, Robert III., was in Dundee on 9th March, 1390, and 7th April, 1392. James I. of Scotland resided at Dundee during the five days that elapsed between his coronation at Scone on 21st May, 1424, and the opening of his first Parliament at Perth. James II. was in Dundee on 5th May, 1457, and James III. was thrice in Dundee in 1464, and signed several important charters.

Dundee seems to have afforded special attractions to the gallant James IV. In the September of the year of his accession, 1488, he resided for seven days at Dundee, and had various costly dresses made for him at that time. Evidently the King "had a high old time" when here, for there were 18 punds Scots paid "to the Frenchmen that played before the King." It is not very clear whether these players were musicians, or mere rope-dancers and "tumblers," as the descriptive words are not very precise.

After this time James IV. visited Dundee annually, and signed many important documents here. On one occasion, in 1494, he had purposed visiting Dundee just after Christmas, and preparations were made for lodging the King in the house of James Rollok in Argyllis-gait (now the Overgate). But the King was suddenly called to the West of Scotland, and a claim was lodged for the expenses incurred.

On 22nd December, 1497, James IV. passed through Dundee on his way from Perth to Aberdeen, and remained for one night in the burgh, taking up his residence in James Rollok's house. In the Accounts of the Lord High Treasurer an entry shows that the King was a munificent "paying guest" according to the rates current at the time:—"Item, to James Rollokis wif, quhar the King lugyit all that nycht, be the Kingis command, xxxj shillings." This house apparently stood on the north side of Overgate, nearly opposite Thorter Row. James Rollok was one of the leading burgesses of the time, and was "Custumar" (Collector of Customs for the King) at that time.

In March, 1497-8, the King remained in Dundee for more than a week, and from that date till 1505 he was an annual visitor.

James V. was more frequently resident in Dundee than any other Scottish monarch. His name first appears as that of a visitor on 6th March, 1519, when he was barely seven years old. He returned thither in March of the following year. Dundee must have had special fascinations for him, as he frequently stayed in the burgh—probably at Dudhope Castle —for a fortnight or three weeks. In 1526-7 he remained here from 9th till 20th February, and in October, 1530, his residence was extended for three weeks.

Every year after this date till his death in 1542 the King visited Dundee, waiting occasionally for a fortnight. In 1540 he passed through Dundee on his way to Edinburgh, and was received by the burgesses with great jubilation. As the record quaintly puts it, he came with the Queen to Dundee, "quhair wes ane coistly entres prepairet for thame," as this was the Queen's first appearance here. It was while the King was at Dundee that he consented to meet his uncle, Henry VIII., at York; and his neglect of this promise ultimately brought about his downfall.

His mother, Margaret Tudor (sister of Henry VIII.), was also a visitor to Dundee, and from here she wrote a remarkable letter to her brother, dated 16th October, 1537, regarding her proposed divorce from her third husband Henry, Lord Methven.

Queen Mary regarded Dundee with special favour. Shortly after her return to Scotland in 1561, she made a Royal Progress through the kingdom, and "wes honourablie ressavit" at Dundee. In 1562, after her successful expedition against the Earl of Huntly, she returned by Dundee, and resided here for several days in November. The Town Council entertained the Queen, and presented a "propyne" or gift of some kind, taking a special tax from the inhabitants to defray the cost.

On the occasion of her next visit to Dundee in September,

1564, she presented to Dundee the orchard formerly belonging to the Franciscan Monastery, to be used as a burial-place, that cemetery being the present Howff of Dundee, which was then described as being outside the burgh boundaries.

In September, 1565, the Queen led an army against the rebel Lords, and wrote at Dundee the letter summoning her people to arms. This was her last visit; but in April, 1567, she showed her goodwill to the burgh by granting the ecclesiastical property of the Catholics, which had been confiscated, to form what is still known as "the Hospital Fund," to be applied to the relief of the poor and for other public purposes.

James VI. was also a frequent visitor to Dundee. In April, 1589, he led an army to the north against Huntly, passing through Dundee at the head of the troops. In 1592, when the King wished to avoid meeting Parliament, he suddenly disappeared, and a contemporary writer tells that he was in hiding at Dundee for eight days.

On two later occasions James VI. marched through Dundee leading an army against the insurgent nobles; and in May, 1597, he attended the meeting of the General Assembly, and held a fierce altercation with Andrew Melville regarding the freedom of the Kirk. He was present at the General Assembly, held at Dundee in March, 1597-98; and he presided at a Privy Council meeting in Dundee on 28th October, 1601, when many of the Royal servants were made burgesses.

In 1617, when the King returned from England to visit his ancient kingdom, he was splendidly entertained at Dundee, remaining for a night at Dudhope Castle, and receiving addresses, Latin poems, and other forms of welcome, prepared by learned Dundonians.

Charles II. was thrice in Dundee upon memorable occasions. In June, 1650, he landed at Aberdeen and proceeded south by way of Kinnaird Castle, Forfarshire, to Dundee on his route to Falkland Palace. The following October witnessed the incident known in history as "the start." The King was at Perth when it was proposed to raise the nobles of Forfarshire to assist his escape. He set out through the Carse of Gowrie, rode in hot haste to Dudhope, and then, accompanied by the Viscount of Dudhope, he passed to Auchterhouse, Cortachy, and Glen Clova; but the plot was discovered, and he was intercepted and brought back to Perth.

On 21st February, 1651, Charles II. was in Dundee as a guest of Lord Balcarres, in whose house he resided. The welcome accorded to him at Dundee brought the vengeance of Cromwell upon the burgh, and was one of the causes of Monck's brutality at the Siege of Dundee in September, 1651.

The Chevalier de St. George (James VIII.) visited Dundee on 6th January, 1716, and remained for some time on horseback at the Cross, in the midst of a snow storm, to receive the homage of his numerous supporters in the burgh. He lodged for the night in the house of Sir George Stewart of Grandtully, which stood on the Castle-hill almost on the site of the Royal British Hotel.

From 1716 until 1844 no British Sovereign visited Dundee. The first of the Hanoverian Dynasty to come here was Queen Victoria, and she was twice in Dundee. On 9th September, 1844, the Queen, Prince Albert, and the Princess Royal set sail from Woolwich in the yacht Victoria and Albert, designing to land at Dundee and pass through the Highlands to Blair Atholl.

Great preparations were made for this event. A temporary triumphal arch was erected at Dundee Docks where the party was to land, its site being now marked by the Royal Arch erected some years afterwards. The town was decorated in honour of Her Majesty, and the reception accorded was very hearty. When returning from Blair Atholl, the Queen again passed through Dundee, embarking at the port on 4th October.

The next visit of the Queen was on 20th June, 1879, when she made her journey southwards by way of the first Tay Bridge, which had been opened for traffic in May of the previous year. Provost Brownlee then presented an address to Her Majesty. On 19th June, 1891, the Queen passed through Dundee on her way from the North, and for the first time made a continuous journey over the Firth of Tay and the Firth of Forth by the two great viaducts.

The Prince and Princess of Wales (afterwards Edward VII. and Queen Alexandra) embarked at Dundee for Copenhagen on 3rd September, 1864; and Queen Alexandra visited Dundee in 1907 and 1910, when on her way to Denmark and Norway. On 10th July, 1914, George V. and Queen Mary visited Dundee with the Princess Mary, and were loyally received.

Mary summons her people

The odd pair turn the heads of passers-by

They're French spies — hang them at the Cross!

MANY will remember the dread of an invasion of this country by the French in 1861, which gave rise to the Volunteer Movement. Great as was the excitement at that time, it could not be compared in intensity to the wave of terror which swept over Great Britain 60 years earlier, when the threatened invasion by Napoleon Bonaparte in 1801 set the whole nation agog with patriotic excitement. Ireland had been somewhat unwillingly united to Great Britain after a protracted campaign against the rebels of 1798; and the embers of revolt were still smouldering there.

In Scotland the landing of "the Mounseers," as they were called, was confidently expected; and the east coast, it was thought, would be the first point attacked. Lunan Bay was named as the spot chosen by Bonaparte for the landing of a great army that was to march upon Edinburgh, while another army, landed at Dover, was to capture London.

Readers of Scott's novel, "The Antiquary" will remember how this exciting period is described, with Fairport (Arbroath) as its centre, and Musselcrag (Auchmithie) as the harbour nearest to Lunan Bay. This expectation of the French spread all along the coast towns of Forfarshire and Fife; and naturally caused distrust of any one who, by eccentricity of garb or outlandishness of speech, betrayed a foreign origin. Dundee, as a seaport easily accessible from the North Sea, was especially subject to fits of suspicion, and the following true story gives a veritable picture of the feelings excited by what was called "the threatened invasion."

There were two American students at Edinburgh University in 1801, named John Bristed and Andrew Cowan. They were both from New York, the former studying law, and the latter medicine; and both afterwards attained distinction, Bristed becoming a barrister of the Inner Temple, and Cowan taking his M.D. degree. Dr. Cowan published a remarkable book in 1803 entitled "Anthropaideia, or a Tractate on General Education;" and Bristed wrote two volumes describing "A Pedestrian Tour through part of the Highlands of Scotland in

K

1801," from which the story of his adventures in Dundee has been taken.

It must be owned that John Bristed is as prosy a literary bore as can be found in the literature of his time. He devotes 75 pages of his introduction to a detailed analysis of Dr. Cowan's "Tractate;" and he intrudes throughout his book numerous long quotations from the classical authors, from Shakespeare, Pope, Samuel Butler, and other English poets, and—most wonderful of all—from Robert Burns, with whose poems, at that early date, he was familiarly acquainted. The adventures of the two travellers on their memorable tour are told with a prolixity that tries the patience of every reader, but the story is valuable as showing the condition of Scotland at a time when tourists were few and the means of travelling were scanty.

At seven o'clock in the morning of 1st August, 1801, John Bristed and Andrew Cowan set forth from Edinburgh in quest of loud and strange adventure. They decided to disguise themselves as sailors, with check shirts, jackets, trousers, and knapsacks, Bristed wearing huge goggles so as further to make himself unrecognisable. They travelled to Leith Pier, their uncouth appearance provoking much laughter, and there they crossed the Firth of Forth, landing at Pettycur, which was then the Fife harbour for the ferry. Thence they proceeded by East Wemyss, Leven, and Largo to St. Andrews, meeting many strange natives of Fife who were much diverted by the costumes and language of the tourists.

At St. Andrews they visited the widow of Principal Joseph M'Cormick, who received them very coldly. They made their way to Dundee Ferry (Newport) without any startling adventures, and entered the pinnace which was to carry them across the Tay. One of their fellow-passengers was Mr. Jonas Watson, "a tobacconist in the town of Dundee, a reputable tradesman, who has a son at Charleston in America in a thriving mercantile business." He advised them to seek lodgings in the inn kept by Peter Cooper at the Shore-head (Fish Street), and immediately on landing at Dundee harbour they made their way to Cooper's place

While they were travelling through Fife, they had an inkling, from the suspicious looks directed towards them, that they were regarded as spies. This suspicion had been confirmed by

Bristed and Cowan frequently disputing upon classical questions and quoting Latin, which the natives mistook for French. These rumours had preceded them to Dundee, and already they were spotted as emissaries of Napoleon, sent out to view the land.

Peter Cooper, "the little consequential hero of the tap," at first was unwilling to have anything to do with these strangely-attired travellers, but Bristed began a flattering oration about the courage, generosity, and hospitality of Scotsmen, and told him a number of brazen lies about the Scottish emigrants who had risen to eminence in America, so Cooper relented, and showed them into "a dark and dismal room upstairs, at one end of which stood two beds in a dreary recess."

Here Bristed began to write up the journal of the tour, and then he and Cowan started a discussion on the comparative merits of Plautus and Terence, quoting Latin copiously. Probably Cooper overheard this lingo, and it confirmed him in the notion that they were two French spies. He suddenly burst into the room, and told them that two gentlemen were below who wished to speak with them. He was directed to show them up to the room, and Bristed's narrative proceeds thus:—

"Soon thereafter entered the room in which we were, a person whose appearance, manner, gesture, and address all declared that he was organized to be a gentleman; he was followed by M——. Mr. Sterling, the gentleman who entered with M——, said,—I beg pardon, gentlemen, for this intrusion, but we are under the unpleasant necessity of troubling you and wounding our own feelings, because no less than four informations have been laid before us as Magistrates, that two strangers of a very suspicious and dangerous appearance were gone into Cooper's public-house.

"Now, at this critical moment, when all the nation is under the alarm and dread of an invasion from our enemies the French, who seem determined to leave nothing untried which fraud can contrive or force can execute in order to effect the ruin of this country, we, who are in a civil capacity, are obliged to be very watchful and circumspect. We have, therefore, taken the liberty of waiting on you, gentlemen, merely to give you an opportunity of declaring who you are, and thereby preventing all occasion of future molestation during your stay in the town of Dundee."

There is probably more of Bristed than of Sterling in this long-winded speech, but it brought the travellers to their bearings. They explained that they were Edinburgh students of American birth on a tour through Scotland; but as they had no papers to confirm their statements, Sterling hesitated. His comrade, M——, was more out-spoken, and stated that they dare not let such suspicious characters go; so Mr. Sterling was forced to send for his clerk that an order might be made to commit Bristend and Cowan to Dundee jail as French spies.

When the clerk came, he was even less credulous than the two Magistrates. He cross-examined them as to the Edinburgh Professors whom the accused knew, and as to other prominent citizens of the metropolis. Bristed replied:—"Sir, I have the honour of being known to Mr. Scott, who lives at 27 Queen Street [he should have said Castle Street], Edinburgh, an intimate and honoured friend of the late celebrated traveller, Abyssinian Bruce. Mr. Scott is a gentleman whom I love as much for the urbanity of his manners and the easy gracefulness of his conversation as I admire and revere him for the respectability and sterling integrity of his character."

It is interesting to find this early tribute of the merits of Sir Walter Scott from the pen of an American admirer; but it was not sufficient to satisfy the clerk. Then Bristed stated:— "I am also acquainted with Mr. Laing, a very respectable bookseller in Edinburgh, who lately purchased a library of books from the King of Denmark, and whose name is known and esteemed throughout the British Empire and on the Continent."

But Laing—the father of the late renowned Dr. David Laing of the Signet Library—was quite unknown to the Dundee worthies. The clerk ordered the accused to show how much money they had, and the smallness of the sum confirmed his suspicions. However, it was arranged that a letter should be written to Laing and this was done accordingly. Then M——, the Magistrate, went out for the constables that the two prisoners might be taken into custody.

While he was gone, Mr. Sterling informed the tourists as to the rumours current in Dundee regarding them. "Some declared that we were French spies, come with a determination to murder all the people in the land; others said we were English deserters, who wished to hide ourselves in Dundee; some insisted upon it that we were Irish rebels, and ought to be hanged on the spot, as a specimen of British justice and an example of Dundee loyalty to the Sovereign of this Empire; others again contented themselves with mercifully insinuating that we were Wandering Jews, and should be put into the round-house for a few days, and then publicly whipt through the town, after which we might be sent about our business."

At length M—— returned with his myrmidons, and was about to carry off the hapless tourists to jail, when Mr. Sterling made a last appeal in their favour. He earnestly asked them if there was no one in Dundee, no medical students, who might know them; but Bristed could recollect no one. So Mr. Sterling determined to bring two Edinburgh students, resident in Dundee, to see the prisoners, on the chance that they might be recognised.

Shortly afterwards Mr. Sterling returned, bringing with him Mr. Patrick Nimmo, formerly a medical student, then settled as a doctor in Dundee, who remembered both Bristed and Cowan; and Mr. Watson, another "medical," came in and confirmed the statement. Bristed produced his diary, and got Sterling to write a certificate in it, which Nimmo and Watson signed. This document is placed on the front page of Bristed's book, and reads thus:—

> "Mr. Bristed and Mr. Cowan, two young gentlemen of America, now students of Medicine at the University of Edinburgh, having been brought before me this evening as suspicious persons, or vagrants, who could give no good account of themselves, did satisfy me of their being what they said they were, by producing two gentlemen of this town, well known to me, who attended the classes along with them, and bear testimony to their characters.
>
> Patrick Nimmo.   Dundee, 7th August, 1801.
> John Watson.   Patrick Sterling, D.L.
>
> By our joint testimony we have delivered from durance vile our two fellow-students."

Here it may be mentioned that Dr. Patrick Nimmo was long the leading physician in Dundee, and survived till July, 1855. Being thus rescued from danger of imprisonment, the two travellers invited Mr. Watson to spend the evening with them. Bristed is not very complimentary to Watson, describing him as "a slender, little boy, about twenty, with nearly as much meaning in his face as is expressed in those blocks of wood which support fashionable head-dressers in the shop windows of milliners and of barbers." Watson went to the Post Office to fetch back the letter which had been written to Mr. Laing.

The advent of the two strangely-attired pedestrians had thoroughly alarmed the inhabitants of Dundee. Watson told them "that all the town had been in an uproar; that men, women, and children were seen issuing out of the doors, hanging half-way out of the windows, and choking up the main street with a press of mortal carcases thronged together, and demanding the immediate execution of the two bloody-minded terrible spies, who were come with an intention to murder all the men, to ravish all the women, and eat up all the children in Dundee." They expected that the two spies "were going to be hanged directly on a gallows made on purpose in the very middle of the principal street in Dundee."

The jovial supper was prolonged till very late, and then Watson took his leave, "first seriously exhorting us to parade the streets of Dundee in the morning; not because the town contained anything particularly worth seeing, but that the sapient and humane inhabitants being all agog with expectation might have their laudable curiosity gratified by staring at two men arrayed in sailor's jackets, and which two men had been taken up the evening before on the well-grounded suspicion of their being two French spies." The tourists, however, did not take Watson's advice. "Just as the town clock struck five in the morning, we deemed it fitting to depart, and therefore set forward for Perth."

It is needless to pursue the two travellers further in their pilgrimage through Scotland. Suffice it to say that John Bristed deserves to be immortalised as one of the most intolerable literary bores who ever put pen to paper. He breaks off in the middle of the record of an incident to deliver a fifty-page disquisition upon "Female Delicacy," "The Education of Women," or stories hardly fitted for ears polite. The world of letters would not have suffered much had John Bristed been hanged as a French spy at the Cross of Dundee!

At the court of our God-fearing Miss Mary

THERE are many forms of amusement in this world, but perhaps one of the strangest twists in the human mind which desires occupation of an unusual kind is that which makes the monomaniac take delight in litigation. It may be a latent love of gambling which tempts the litigant to plunge into law-suit after law-suit, revelling in "the glorious uncertainty of law;" or it may be the revolt of an independent spirit against some real or fancied injustice. Whatever may be its cause, the fact is undeniable that when the habit of having law-suits is formed it exercises a fascination as powerful and as destructive as laudanum-drinking or opium-smoking.

Scott refers in "Redgauntlet" to the inveterate litigant "poor Peter Peebles" as one of this class, and this character was a real personage, upon whose case the novelist was once himself employed as counsel.

Another veritable devotee of "a guid gangin' plea" was Andrew Nicol, who flourished—if that be the proper word—about 1792, and tasted all the sweets and bitters of the law's delays. He was a Kinross weaver, who claimed to have a right over a portion of ground upon which his neighbour had encroached; and for years Nicol put in motion, at great expense, all the ponderous machinery of the law to vindicate his rights, though the cost of a single action was more than he could have gained by a judgment in his favour.

Some eighty years ago a popular song was current, in which the fancied delights of the law were detailed, and one of the verses ran thus:—

>If you're fond of pure vexation,
>And long procrastination,
>You're just in a situation
>   To enjoy a suit at law.

Complaints against the law, however, are not of modern origin. About 350 years ago Sir David Lyndsay of the Mount humorously described the delays and dangers of the law in the quaint language of his period. The speaker had given the loan of a mare to his neighbour to cart coals, but by accident the mare was drowned at the quarry. The owner applied to the Consistory Court, and was baffled and perplexed for two years by diverse law processes, as thus detailed:—

THE LOST MARE.

Marie! I lent my gossip my meare to fetch hame coils,
And he hir drounit into the Querrell hollis;
And I ran to the Cousistorie to pleinye,
And thair I happinit amang ane greidie meinye;
They gave me first ane thing they call *Citandum,*
Within aucht dayis I gat bot *Lybellandum,*
Within ane month I gat *Ad Opponendum,*
In half ane yeir I gat *Interloquendum,*
And syne I gat, how call ye it?—*Ad Replicandum,*
Bot I could nevir ane word yit understand him;
And than they gart me cast out mony plackis,
And gart me pay for four-and-twentie Actis;
Bot or thay came half gait to *Concludendum,*
The Fiend ane plack was left for to defend him.
Thus they postponit me twa yeir, with thair traine,
Syne *Hodie ad octo* bade me cum againe;
And than thir ruiks they roupit wonder fast,
For sentence-silver they cryit at the last.
Of *Pronunciandum* they maid me wonder fain,
—Bot I gat never my gude grey meare again!

One old Scottish proverb declares that "Law licks up a'," and another gives the sound advice, "Law's costly; tak' a pint and 'gree." But all this condensed wisdom has not prevented the confirmed litigant from finding supreme delight in a succession of lawsuits. The late Sir Robert Menzies, Bart., was a notable example of this curious habit. For half a century before his death he was hardly ever without a case in progress in the Court of Session. The story of a Dundee lady who suffered from a similar mania for law is now to be related.

Mary Ritchie was the daughter of Alexander Ritchie, a

prosperous shoemaker in Dundee, and was born there in 1789. Her father died when she was quite a girl, leaving what was then considered a large fortune at her disposal; but Miss Ritchie was no sluggard, willing to live at ease upon the fruit of her father's industry. She had inherited acute business faculties from her parent, and before she was out of her teens she had entered into partnership with her friend, Miss Easson, and established a drapery concern, to which she devoted all her energies.

The business flourished exceedingly, so much so that before she had reached her fortieth year she was able to retire from active life, having made over £10,000, in addition to her father's legacy. It is related that when she was asked by a friend why she had retired while her powers were unimpaired, she replied that "she made that muckle siller that she was fear'd the Lord wad turn against her!" In this answer there may be found a trace of the religious feeling which afterwards produced one of the strangest incidents in her long life.

The retiral of Miss Ritchie from business had the unfortunate effect of turning her energies into another and more dangerous channel. It appears that when she was winding up the affairs of the drapery shop a dispute arose between her and her partner, the details of which need not here be given. Suffice it to say that from the Sheriff Court it was taken to the Court of Session, and after a protracted trial Miss Ritchie gained a decision in her favour.

Even yet the famous case of "Ritchie versus Easson" is quoted as having laid down a principle in commercial law; and of this fact Miss Ritchie was extremely proud. Her experience in the Courts, however, had infected her with the legal mania, and of that disease she was never afterwards cured.

Some ladies find their chief solace in the society of ministers; but Miss Ritchie preferred to spend her time and money with the lawyers. She became quite an expert amateur lawyer, and could "knap law" as glibly as Bartoline Saddletree in "The Heart of Midlothian." But that "Redgauntlet" was published in 1824, while the great case of Ritchie versus Easson did not reach the Court of Session till 1827, one might almost think that Scott had it in his mind when describing a curiously similar case in that novel:—

Peter Peebles and Paul Plainstanes entered into partnership in the year —— as mercers and linen-drapers, in the Lucken-booths, and carried on a great line of business to mutual advantage. But the learned counsel needeth not to be told, societias est mater discordiarum, partnership often makes pleaship. The company being dissolved by mutual consent in the year ——, the affairs had to be wound up, and after certain attempts to settle the matter, it was at last brought into the Court, and has branched out into several distinct processes, most of whilk have been conjoined by the Ordinary. It is to the state of these processes that counsel's opinion is particularly directed. There is the original action of Peebles v. Plainstanes, convening him for payment of £3000, less or more, as alleged balance due by Plainstanes. Secondly, there is a counter-action, in which Plainstanes is pursuer and Peebles defender, for £2500, less or more, being balance alleged, per contra, to be due by Peebles. Thirdly, Mr. Peebles's seventh agent advised an action of compt and reckoning at his instance, wherein what balance should prove due on either side might be fairly struck and ascertained. Fourthly, to meet the hypothetical case, that Peebles might be found reliable in a balance to Plainstanes, Mr. Wildgoose, Mr. Peebles's eighth agent, recommended a multiplepoinding to bring all parties concerned into the field.

Fortunately, in one sense, Miss Ritchie won her cause in the Court of Session, though not before she had changed her lawyers as frequently as did Peter Peebles. She became an adept at discovering clever young lawyers, and though she was frugal in the matter of fees, her cases often gave splendid opportunities for distinction.

Though Mary Ritchie had remained single until past her 40th year, she did not despair of meeting a lover, or at least securing a husband. No doubt she had faith in her fortune as a sure means of attracting a prospective husband, for she would be familiar with the verse :—

   Be a lassie ne'er sae black,
    Gin she hae the penny siller,
   Set her upo' Tintock tap,
    The wind'll blaw a man till her.

But she had learned enough of law, she thought, to protect herself against the wiles of unscrupulous fortune-hunters. She therefore directed her Dundee lawyer, for the time being, to draw up a marriage contract in due form, providing for the settlement of her fortune upon herself and her children (if any), and only leaving the name and description of her future husband blank, to be filled up when he came on the scene and she accepted him. Curiously enough, this very legal document became a fruitful source of litigation for many years.

Having some distant relatives at Leamington, Warwickshire, Miss Ritchie left Dundee and settled there about 1832. Here she met a certain Mr. Alcock, wood merchant, whom she accepted as her husband, and whose name filled up the blank in the fatal marriage contract. But alas! Fortune did not smile upon her long-delayed nuptials. Apparently the husband desired to have more control of his wife's fortune than the strict terms of the deed permitted; and Mrs. Alcock's reverence for the law drove her into open rebellion. She deserted her husband, returned to Dundee, and then raised a suit in Chancery against him, demanding restitution of some of her money which he had obtained.

In those dismal days there was no Married Women's Property Act to protect the wife's property after marriage; and evidently Mr. Alcock did not think that the ante-nuptial contract which he had signed was binding upon him. In any case, the lady entered upon a new and varied course of legal experiences, with London as the scene of action instead of Edinburgh. Mrs. Alcock's name soon came to be as well known in the Court of Chancery as that of another distinguished lady of a later time, who prosecuted and persecuted the late Charles Gounod, the composer, for many years. In recording her career at this time, a local journalist remarks :—

After nursing her Dundee property for a time, she used to go off to London whenever she had two or three hundred pounds to spare, to have another spell of law, and to urge on her case. Her appetite for litigation grew by what it fed on; and, being in a position which enabled her to enjoy that expensive luxury, she did not stint herself of her peculiar enjoyment.

It became a special pleasure for her to take her case out of one Dundee lawyer's hands and put it in the charge of another. Then the first task of the new agent was to fight against his predecessor's bill for legal expenses, a duel which always afforded her particular delight. The proverb declares that "he who is his own lawyer has a fool for his client." Mrs. Alcock was by no means a fool, but she had to pay very dear for her whistle. Many of the young Dundee lawyers who had to do with her cases afterwards gained eminent positions in the local legal profession.

There is always some compensating defect even in the most perfect character. One might have thought that so keen, hard-headed, and practical a woman as Mrs. Alcock was would have been least susceptible of religious emotion. And yet she became an ardent disciple of the latest "revelation" vouchsafed to mankind in the form of the Mormon Bible, by the hands of the Prophet, Joseph Smith.

It was early in the "forties" that the first Mormon Apostle reached Dundee in the person of the famous Orson Pratt, known among the faithful as "the Philosopher." He had the gift of oratory, a striking appearance, and a fluency of utterance that could awaken enthusiasm. In those remote days polygamy was never mentioned in this country in connection with Mormonism;—indeed, it was not until "Saintly Pilgrims" reached Utah that this form of social life was openly followed.

To the religionists with a tendency to emotion the new doctrine of Mormonism seemed but a revival of the Pentecostal grace that had attended the ministrations of John Wesley, George Whitfield, and other enthusiasts, who had succeeded in rousing the people from the torpor of indifferentism. In fact, the Mormon Apostle of 1840-50 was in many respects an anticipation of the modern Revivalist.

Orson Pratt was so successful by his street-corner preaching that he gathered a goodly number of followers in Dundee. Their meeting-place at first was in the Hammerman's Hall, Barrack Street, now part of Mr. Buchan's hall; and at a later date the Mormon Church assembled in the Wrights' Hall, Key's Close, in the Nethergate—one of the old closes swept away by the recent improvements. Many converts in Dundee and Arbroath ultimately made their way to Salt Lake City, the Home of the Saints.

How Mrs Alcock came under the influence of the Mormon preachers is not known. It is possible that as she lived just opposite their meeting-place in Barrack Street she may have been tempted to go into the Hall, and there her heart may have responded to the appeals of the enthusiasts.

One of the Dundee converts, Mr. Stenhouse, rose to eminence among the Mormons at Utah; and it is not unlikely that Mrs. Alcock was known to him. The wife of Elder Stenhouse—Fanny Stenhouse—after some experience of Utah, abandoned Mormonism, and published an exposure of it, in 1880, under the title "An Englishwoman in Utah;" but long before that time Mrs. Alcock had passed away, and apparently she believed to the last that Utah was the Promised Land, and that Salt Lake City was the New Jerusalem.

Alongside this religious sentiment on her part, there persisted the old craze for litigation. In her later years, when an old, bent woman, far past the allotted span, she might be seen laboriously wending her way up Barrack Street towards the Sheriff Court-house, carrying her bag with its precious load of documents, and rejoicing as much to hear her name in the Court as though she were thus receiving high honour.

Her death took place in her Barrack Street house on 6th September, 1869, when in her 80th year. She had no immediate relatives to heir the large fortune which she left, and which long years of litigation had not exhausted.

Whipped through the streets 13 times in the name of Justice

EVERY one acquainted with the social history of Scotland knows that in early times the lash was frequently used for the punishment of aggravated offences. It will not surprise the reader to be told that previous to the Reformation, and long subsequent to it, offenders were publicly scourged in the market-place of Dundee; but it may startle many to learn that only 100 years ago a criminal was driven through the principal streets of Dundee, tied to the tail of a cart, and scourged in public by the common hangman. Yet this is a fact gravely noted in the newspapers of the time, and was regarded as much a matter of course by the reporters of the period as the recording at the present day of a small fine for drunkenness or riotous conduct.

The last instance of public scourging in Dundee took place in May, 1824, and was witnessed by a vast assemblage. To show that this incident was a survival of an old custom, only obsolete in recent years, it is sufficient to turn to the early records of the burgh. In an interesting chapter entitled "Offences and Their Punishments," the late Bailie Alexander Maxwell gives much curious information in his book, "Old Dundee Prior to the Reformation."

In the sixteenth century the usual punishment for theft— or "pickery," as it was called—was banishment from the town. It may be doubted whether the exclusion of a thief beyond the limits of the burgh would tend to his reformation, or would in any way protect the unfortunate outsiders who were not Dundonians from his depredations. Yet there are several cases recorded in the Burgh Court books in which women convicted of theft were banished, and compelled to take their children with them.

In cases of aggravated theft the offenders were scourged at the market-place before being exiled. It is recorded that in 1523 a certain Anne Butchart, who had wrongfully taken the wort belonging to a maltman, was "ordainit to be scurgit."

A very strange case occurred at Dundee in 1552. Two thieves, Wattie Firsell and Duncan Robertson, had set upon a poor woman under silence of night, and had robbed her. They were both convicted, and the sentence of the Bailie was "that Duncan sall scurge Wattie round about within the bounds of this burgh, as use is, and gif he fails in the extreme punishment of Wattie, then Climas, the hangman, sall scurge them baith in his maist extreme manner he can. And thereafter Wattie to be had to the Cross, and, be open proclamation, banishit this burgh for seven years." No doubt the fear of the "hangman's whip" would make Duncan Robertson lay on the lash with might and main.

The abandoned wretch who combined theft with sacrilege received little mercy from the Reformers. Mr. Maxwell tells how that at the time when the fiery eloquence of John Knox and other Reformers was crowding St. Mary's Church with worshippers, a thief took the opportunity of plying his vocation there, for which he was condignly punished. The judgment was in these terms:—"The Bailies ordain Alex. Smyth to be scurgit through this burgh, and banisht the same forever, and never to be fund thereintil, under the pain of deid; because, being apprehended with pickery and theft this last Sunday in the kirk, he confessit the same, and submitted himself in the will of the Bailies; wha declarit the same as is above specifeit."

When women were banished from the town, it was usually declared that the punishment of their return without leave should be death by drowning.

In course of time the rigour of the law was tempered, and offences at one time visited with extreme punishment were condoned by fine instead of imprisonment. That much-abused local hero, John Graham of Claverhouse, was one of the first to propose that clemency should be extended to minor offences. When Graham was Provost of Dundee he presented a petition to the Privy Council, suggesting that some of the prisoners in the Tolbooth should be subjected to fine rather than to incarceration for minor offences; and this application seems to have had some effect, as there was a marked improvement in the method of dealing with such prisoners.

It is not generally known that England and Scotland differ very much in the power of inflicting the death-penalty. While in England only two crimes—treason and murder—are punishable by death, in Scotland, what are called "the four pleas of the Crown"—murder, robbery, rape, and fire-raising—are still liable to the extreme penalty of the law, though usually the Prosecutor only asks for capital punishment in cases of murder. The case now to be narrated belongs to one of these four offences.

On the evening of 5th May, 1822, while a young girl, Margaret Miller, aged 14 years, was going along the road from Dundee to Glamis, she was attacked by two men and criminally assaulted. John Miller and William Storrier were apprehended and accused of the crime. They declared their innocence, but both men were committed for trial. They were brought to the Perth Circuit Court held on 13th September, 1822. The presiding Judges were Lord Hermand (George Fergusson) and Lord Succoth (Ilay Campbell).

The prisoners put in a plea of "Not guilty," and as the evidence was of a special kind, the trial was conducted with closed doors. A considerable number of witnesses (including the girl) were examined for the prosecution, while many of the witnesses for the defence testified to the good character of the accused. The Prosecutor, Mr. John Hope (afterwards Lord Justice-Clerk), withdrew that part of the accusation which would have involved the death-punishment, and limited the case to one of assault.

In defending the prisoners, their advocate, Mr. Thomson, took up a special line of defence. Having described the position of the Glamis Road near the present site of Fairmuir, Mr. Thomson maintained that there could not have been sufficient light at the time the offence was committed to enable the girl to identify her assailants. Here Lord Succoth interposed, and produced an almanack to prove that on the evening of 5th May there was a full moon—a piece of evidence which had been overlooked by the Prosecutor.

When it is remembered that the venerable Judge at this time was 88 years of age—he died the following year—it will be seen that his faculties were as clear and his reasoning as keen as when he was engaged in the Great Douglas Cause nearly sixty years before. The production of the almanack demolished the theory for the defence.

The jury retired, and after a short time returned presenting a written verdict by which they found the prisoners guilty of "assault with intent." The sentence of the Court was that the prisoners should be "detained in the Jail of Dundee till Friday, 4th October, and on that day at 12 o'clock noon, to be publicly whipped by the common hangman, and afterwards transported for 14 years."

This case had caused not a little sensation in Dundee, especially as similar crimes had been perpetrated within a recent date in the neighbourhood. It was thought that the revival of the old form of punishment might deter others from offences of the kind, even though the extreme penalty of death had not been exacted.

When the hour for the execution of the sentence approached, on Friday, 4th October, a vast crowd assembled in the High Street, filling the open space from the Trades Hall in the east, to the Union Hall at the west, and blocking the main thoroughfares of Overgate, Nethergate, Seagate, and Murraygate. As it was the usual market day, many of the farmers and farm-servants had come into the town to witness the unusual spectacle. It was calculated that not less than 10,000 persons were congregated in the open square and side streets.

As the hour of noon struck on the clock of the Town House, a cart was driven up to the piazza, and the prisoners were brought down from the upper cells, as the "Dundee Advertiser" reporter states, "in the humiliating manner usual on such occasions." Their backs were bared, their hats slouched over their faces, and a cord was run round their waists and fastened to the cart. The hangman was there in his official capacity, bearing his dreaded "cat-o'-nine-tails."

In this ignominious manner the melancholy procession started from the front of the Town House, the crowd making way for the cart as it moved slowly along towards the Seagate. Here at the corner of the Trades Hall, nearly opposite the top of Castle Street, the first stop was made, and the hangman administered three stripes to each of the culprits. Then the cart proceeded solemnly on its way. It went along the Seagate to St. Andrew's Street; up that thoroughfare, turning by the Cowgate into the Murraygate, and thus back to the High Street, amid the hooting and derision of the mob. Thence it started on its westward route, by the Overgate, down Tay

Street, and returning by the Nethergate to the Town House. At every corner the cart was stopped and the hangman performed his office.

Thirteen times in the course of the journey did the officer apply the lash, thus making up the Scriptural number of "forty stripes less one." Then the culprits, with lacerated and bleeding bodies, were taken back to the Tolbooth cells, to await the remainder of their sentence of fourteen years' transportation. Here these wretches drop out of history. Probably both of them fill nameless graves at Botany Bay.

The circumstances of the case narrated make it of special interest. Seldom were there two accomplices punished in this ignominious fashion, though the sentence was carried out two years later upon a single prisoner. On 14th May, 1824, a man named Webster, convicted of assault and robbery, was publicly whipped through the streets, and an immense concourse of people witnessed the infliction of the degrading punishment. After having made a tour of the principal streets at the rear of the cart, and receiving the number of lashes decreed, the offender was committed to prison to complete his sentence.

Webster's case was a peculiar one. He was tried for assault at the Perth Circuit Court in April, 1821, and sentenced to twelve months' imprisonment and five years' banishment from Scotland, with the penalty of public whipping should he return before the expiry of his exile. He was captured on 1st May, 1824, and charged with assaulting several people in the east end of Dundee. As he was identified, he had to endure the punishment of whipping. On this occasion the hangman did not officiate. On the previous Saturday an official had been brought from Edinburgh to Arbroath for the purpose of executing a similar sentence upon Robert Sim, a farm-servant who had attempted to murder his sweetheart. No such exhibition of justice had taken place in Arbroath for fifty years, and great crowds assembled to witness it. The Magistrates of Dundee engaged the Edinburgh scourger to officiate in Webster's case.

This was the last instance of public scourging in Dundee. The Police Act, which received the Royal Assent on 24th June, 1824, introduced new methods of punishment, and whipping ceased to be the custom.

At the beginning of last century the stealing of yarn was made liable in Dundee to an extreme penalty. This was, no doubt, an example of class legislation, for the merchants and manufacturers were the administrators of the law. The embezzlement and reset of stolen yarn were punished by a fine of £20, and failing in the payment of this fine the culprits were decreed to be "publicly whipped at the Market-Cross of the burgh." In the "Dundee Advertiser" for 12th July, 1805, there is a list of 18 persons—13 women and 5 men— who were then underlaying this sentence, which had been imposed by that eminent local philanthropist, Justice Blair, "in terms of the Act of Parliament." There is no record in the newspapers of the time as to whether the prisoners paid the fines or endured the scourging, but the fact of the sentence having been pronounced is beyond dispute.

Whipped through town!

Fair Day in Dundee

Highway robbery and mayhem in Scotland's crime capital — Dundee

DUNDONIANS who are privileged to live in these law-abiding times, when every citizen may walk the crowded streets with little fear of personal violence, can have no adequate idea of the dangers braved by their predecessors before the present police system had been developed. One has only to turn to the early numbers of the "Dundee Advertiser" from 1801 till the middle of the last century to notice how crime was rampant and unchecked, and how dangerous it was for the most peaceful citizen to venture forth unarmed after dark. For many years the "Advertiser" strongly advocated the establishment of a regular police force for the protection of the inhabitants; but the old system was maintained, and the Commissioners of Police had not power to establish a force of constables sufficient to preserve good order in the burgh.

The style of "watching and warding," which had been in use from the sixteenth century, and under which every burgess had to take his turn of patrolling a given district, survived in a slightly altered form till the nineteenth century. It was not, indeed, till 1833-4, in the reign of William IV., that the "Act to enable Burghs in Scotland to establish a general System of Police" (known as the Lindsay Act) came into force; and from that time may be dated the beginning of the great improvement in civic rule which we now enjoy. It took considerable time for this reform to show itself; indeed, in Dundee, for some strange reason, several of the Town Councillors persistently opposed the adoption of the Lindsay Act.

Dundee had an unenviable reputation so far as crime was concerned even up till the middle of last century. About from 1830 till 1850 there was no Scottish burgh where robbery and assault were so common; though the more serious crime of murder was comparatively rare. Among the Scottish

R

Judges the name of Dundee became a byword for all that was objectionable. In his "Circuit Journeys" Lord Cockburn makes a remarkable statement regarding Perth Circuit of April, 1852, which shows how Dundee was regarded:—
"Only one case, but a most brutal one, remained, and in a couple of hours it ended in transportation for life. I need scarcely say that it came from Dundee, certainly now, and for many years past, the most blackguard place in Scotland. Perth and its shire are always remarkably innocent. Nearly the whole guilt at this place proceeds from the two counties of Fife and Forfarshire, and, of course, chiefly from their towns. Of these towns, Kirkcaldy, Cupar, and Montrose seem well-behaved enough. Arbroath is not good; Dunfermline (always meaning the district) very bad; Dundee a sink of atrocity, which no moral flushing seems capable of cleansing. A Dundee criminal, especially if a lady, may be known, without any evidence about character, by the intensity of the crime, the audacious bar air, and the parting curses. What a set of she-devils were before us! Mercy on us! If a tithe of the subterranean execration that they launched against us, after being sentenced, was to be as effective as they wished it, commination never was more cordial."

This remark was made nearly twenty years after the Police Act had been adopted, and when there was a regular Police Force organised in Dundee. How much more aptly could it have been applied to the state of Dundee in the first quarter of last century.

From 1822 till about 1840 there was an association of marauders known as "The Black Band" which kept the whole burgh in terror. The secret history of this Society was never fully discovered. It was supposed that the leading members met in an underground cellar in one of the Overgate slums; that they were sworn to secrecy; and that there they planned assaults, robberies, and house-breakings in various parts of the town, assigning the execution of the crimes to certain of their number.

The general plan adopted was to have a crime committed in the east end one week and in the west end the succeeding week, so that the criminals might not be easily localised. Week after week there were accounts of their depredations published in the local papers; and though malefactors were occasionally captured who might be members of the Black Band, they were true to their vows, and did not betray their associates. This seems liker a story of the Vehmgericht in Germany, of the mysterious Council of Ten in Venice, of the Carbonari and the Mafia in Italy of more recent times, than of a staid Scottish burgh in the nineteenth century; but it is a sober fact that such an organisation existed in Dundee about a hundred years ago, and exercised a terrorism over the inhabitants only equal to that of the modern Sicilian brigands.

The dispersal of the Black Band is as mysterious as its origination. It is probable, however, that the deeds now to be narrated were perpetrated by the last survivors of the company; and the year 1840 witnessed the extinction of an association that was a menace to peace and security.

In the year 1839 there was a perfect epidemic of lawlessness in Dundee. House-breakings, thefts, assaults, and robberies with violence were of almost daily occurrence. The well-to-do citizens who had occasion to traverse the dimly-lighted streets at night were forced to carry pistols for their own defence; and it was no uncommon event for a merchant to be attacked even in the High Street by disguised and masked ruffians, who insolently demanded his purse or his life.

On 8th November, 1839, two men entered the shop of Mr. Sinclair, ironmonger, Nethergate, and wished to purchase a pair of pistols. Agnes Mills, the girl in charge, was alarmed by the forbidding aspect of one of the men, and she refused to let him have the desired weapons. From this place the two men went to Mr. Watson's shop in the High Street, and there they managed to obtain the firearms. As already explained, it was usual at that time for citizens to carry pistols for self-defence, and thus the men obtained their wish without much difficulty.

That same evening while Andrew Neave, wright, Dundee, was returning homewards along the Coupar Angus Road, about three miles from his house, he was set upon by two men clad in moleskin, who threatened to shoot him if he did not deliver up all the money he had. He resisted, but was overpowered, and the robbers took from him by violence, five shillings in silver, twopence halfpenny in copper, and half-an-ounce of tobacco. This was poor spoil, and the thieves planned a more daring escapade for the following night.

During the afternoon of Friday these two men were walking through the crowd of farmers congregated in the High Street —that being market day—when they met James Goodlet, a flax-dresser, with whom they were acquainted. The three men loitered about for some time, and noticed the farmers paying and receiving money. One of them remarked, "It's a confounded pity to see them with so much money, and us with so little." The other retorted that if the man would hold his tongue he would put them on a plan to get money. They then went down the Vault, and both men urged Goodlet to join them in attacking and robbing the farmers, saying that they would have sticks and pistols, and would kill their victims rather than be detected. This terrified Goodlet, and he refused to go with them. The two men afterwards met another acquaintance, Fergus Bowie, and strove to induce him to accompany them on a robbing expedition, but he also declined to take part in their enterprise.

The 9th of November was a busy night with the two malefactors. Armed with their loaded pistols they went out on the Old Glamis Road, about three miles from Dundee, and concealed themselves behind a hedge to await some unwary traveller. Robert Smith, sawyer, an aged man, was wending homewards to Dundee about eight o'clock, when the two miscreants dashed out upon him. They both gripped him, one on each side, and demanded his money or his life, for, if he made any resistance, he was a dead man. One of them presented a cocked pistol at his head.

Alarmed by this action, Smith took a shilling out of his pocket and gave it to one of them, saying he was a poor man, and that was all the money he had. But the assailant swore that Smith had more money than that, and holding him backward, he rifled Smith's pockets and found other five shillings. In his waistcoat pocket the robber found two pairs of spectacles. He made the callous remark that he had no use for these, and handed them back contemptuously to Smith. They then made off towards Dundee.

Ere they had gone far they overtook William Sprunt, cloth

lapper, Dundee. One of the robbers seized him, pinioned his arms behind his back, and threatened to shoot him if he did not deliver up all his money. A loaded pistol was held against Sprunt's forehead, one arm was released, and he then took a few shillings out of his pocket and gave them to his captors. Disbelieving Sprunt's statement, one of them thrust his hand into the pocket of Sprunt, and took out the remainder of his money, being fourteen shillings in all. They also took a knife, a pipe-pick, a tobacco pouch, and three halfpence in copper, leaving the luckless cloth lapper "poor indeed." Shortly afterwards old Smith overtook Sprunt, and they condoled together on their misfortune.

The adventures of the night were not yet ended. The spoils that the robbers had obtained were not sufficient to satisfy them. As they came towards Dundee by the Dens Road they overtook Mr. James Lamb, a respected manufacturer (grandfather of the late Mr. A. C. Lamb), who was going to his house in Lamb's Lane, off Bucklemaker Wynd (now Victoria Road). Each seized an arm of their intended victim, and made the customary demand, "Your money or your life," presenting a pistol at his head. Mr. Lamb was wiry and vigorous, and after a brief and noisy struggle, he wrenched himself free from his assailants, and sped towards Lamb's Lane. He had not covered much ground ere he heard a pistol shot, but he did not interrupt his course, and when he reached his house he found that his hat was perforated in two places by bullets which had narrowly missed terminating his career.

This defeat seems to have goaded the two wretches to desperation. They made their way through Dundee and went out the Perth Road, expecting to entrap some late wanderer on this fateful Saturday night. On the lonely part of the road beyond "The Sinderance" they overtook Ogilvie Anderson, wright, who was making his way westward to his home in Longforgan. They seized him, rifled his pockets, and found to their chagrin that he had only two halfpennies in copper, a pencil, and an iron punch, of all of which they relieved him. The produce of their robberies and attempted murder that night only amounted to a few coppers over twenty shillings, and for this paltry sum they "had put their craigs in peril."

When these cases of robbery with violence were reported to

the police, extra precautions were taken. Patrols were sent out to watch Dens Road and Downfield district, and the culprits, knowing that these places were under supervision, transferred their sphere of operations. They did nothing from Saturday night till the following Thursday, 14th November. On that evening James Robertson, servant to the miller of Knapp, was returning from Dundee to Knapp, in the Carse of Gowrie, with a cart laden with slates.

When opposite the Market Muir of Longforgan two fellows started forward from the side of the road, and one of them seized the reins of the horse. The other got up on the cart, and, presenting a pistol, demanded the driver's money. He happened to have £50 in his pocket-book, which he had received at Dundee for meal; but he managed to drop the pocket-book, unperceived, among the slates. He then handed over £2 10s. in silver, which he had loose in his pocket. The one thief asked the other if he would take the man's watch; but they both went off without molesting Robertson further, little dreaming of the prize they had lost.

On the following evening (Friday, 18th November) the two confederates again shifted their quarters, taking up their station on the Coupar Angus Road near Birkhill. That evening about seven o'clock Peter Bell, farmer, Cransley, was riding home from Dundee. When about a mile from Lochee, at a lonely part of the road opposite the Camperdown plantation, two men ran towards him, and one seized the bridle of his horse, demanding his money. Mr. Bell refused, and the other villain struck him a severe blow on the head with a "grievous crab-tree cudgel."

The farmer was a very powerful man, and courageous even against odds. He cried out, "You blackguards, what do you mean by that? If I was off my horse I would do for you!" He then leaped to the ground, and though he had nothing in his hand but his whip, he defended himself boldly against the bludgeon of his assailant. But he was forced to let go the bridle, and he drove his opponent backwards. At this moment the other robber drew out a pistol and fired at the farmer. The horse, terrified by the shot, reared up and bolted along the road. Mr. Bell pursued the animal for a short distance, and when he turned round he saw that the two men had fled.

One of Lord Camperdown's gamekeepers, who had heard

the shot, now came up to Mr. Bell, and they made a search for the miscreants, but no trace could be found of them. The horse was returned to him next day. That same night, about eleven o'clock, as John Walker, fish-cadger, Carnoustie, was returning homeward with his horse and cart, he was stopped by the two men in Arbroath Road. They presented pistols at his head, and demanded his money, but he raised an alarm, crying "Murder! Robbery!" and the men made off. Their three attempts at highway robbery on these two nights had only brought them about thirty-four shillings.

On Thursday, 21st November, Mr. Watson, the ironmonger who had sold the brace of pistols, recognised the two men who had purchased them going along Thorter Row to the Overgate, and pointed them out to the police. They were apprehended, and found to be David Peter, blacksmith, Scouringburn, and John Smith, weaver, Lawson's Close, Overgate. Both were recognised as active Chartists. Peter was an especially repulsive-looking man, but Smith had an innocent air and a plausible manner. They were charged with eight separate offences of highway robbery under aggravating circumstances.

On Friday, 19th February, 1840, they were brought up for trial at Perth Justiciary Court, before Lords Meadowbank, Cockburn, and Medwyn. The prosecutor was the Solicitor-General, Thomas Maitland of Dundrennan (afterwards Lord Dundrennan), and the prisoners were defended by James Moncrieff (afterwards Lord Moncrieff). The trial lasted for seven hours. Both pleaded not guilty at first; but before the evidence was begun, Smith withdrew his plea and pleaded guilty as art and part.

After witnesses on both sides had been heard, Mr. Moncrieff asked that Peter might be allowed to plead again, when he pleaded guilty. In Scotland the statutory punishment for highway robbery at that time was death; but the Solicitor-General only asked for an arbitrary punishment, and the prisoners were both sentenced to transportation for life.

Lord Medwyn (who was the father of the late Bishop Forbes) stated that this was the most remarkable and aggravated case of robbery and attempt at robbery he had ever heard of since he sat on the Bench. Certainly, in their own rude and sordid way, these two men were as daring highwaymen as the famous Dick Turpin himself.

A regular list naming killed and wounded — and this was Fair Day!

FROM the remote period when burgh life in Scotland first appears, the fairs held in the burghs have been of great importance. These fairs formed the chief occasions upon which the inhabitants had dealings with the outside world. At the weekly markets, when the farmers from the neighbourhood brought their produce into the burgh for sale, a slight charge was made on the seller in the form of market dues, to be paid to the Superior of the burgh, whether he was, as in Glasgow and St. Andrews, the Archbishop; or the Baron, as in Kirriemuir and Greenock; or the Constable, as in Dundee.

These Fairs, which at first were held only once a year, were times of primitive Free Trade. For a day, or a week, according to the terms of the Burgh Charter, it was lawful for strangers and "unfreemen" to enter the burgh, and to sell their "fremit" (foreign) wares to the inhabitants in the Market-gait as freely as though they were born or regularly admitted burgesses. At all other times there was strict Protection extended to the "toun's bairns," for no foreigner dared enter the Market-place to offer his wares, under pain of expulsion and confiscation of his goods.

The Fairs, which were in most burghs arranged to fall on the Patron Saint's Day, in pre-Reformation times were like the Carnival—full and free licence from normal limitations. A quaint old Scottish term was applied to those travelling merchants who went from Fair to Fair. They were known as "dustifuttit men"—wayfarers who could not shake the dust off their feet as a witness against the burghs that would not receive them. As the history of the Fairs in Dundee fairly represents what happened in other burghs, the following notice may be taken as typical:—

St. Clement, the Sailor's Saint, had been the patron-saint of Dundee until the close of the twelfth century, when the miraculous salvation from shipwreck of David, Earl of Huntingdon (brother of King William the Lion) led him to dedicate the New Church to the Blessed Virgin Mary, who thus became protectress. Consequently the Fair of Dundee was held on Assumption Day of Marymas, 15th August, which was known originally as Our Lady Fair, and is still called, by a curious corruption of terms, "Lady Mary Fair."

About the fourteenth century a second Fair was instituted by the Scrymgeoures, Constables of Dundee, on the Nativity of the Virgin, 8th September, old style (now 19th September), and this was known as "the Latter Fair." In documents of the period from 1550 to 1600 these two Fairs are frequently indicated.

Some time in the early eighteenth century an additional Fair was instituted. Its origin is obscure, but as it was held on the spot of ground known as "Stobs Muir," then about a mile and a half outside the burgh boundaries, it came to be known as "Stobs Fair." The name may have been derived from the fact that a wooden (or "stob") cross stood on the site of this muir, on the north-east highway to Dundee; just as in Glasgow the "Stob Cross" stood at the western access to the burgh, and has now given a name to a wide district.

In any case, it is beyond dispute that at the beginning of the nineteenth century Stobs Fair had been so long in existence that it had gained an unenviable notoriety as a place where the riotous conduct of the frequenters recalled the unbridled licence of the Continental Carnival.

Similar references in successive years show that Stobs Fair was anticipated as a time when lawlessness was rampant, and when the Fair was recognised, as in Roman times, as a period when a saturnalia of pent-up energy might have free course.

A tragic occurrence took place at Stobs Fair in July, 1809. At that time, while Press-gangs were forcibly carrying off men to serve in the navy, there were recruiting parties sent to every Fair for the purpose of enlisting the sturdy agriculturists who attended these gatherings, so that the army, which had suffered during the Napoleonic Wars, might be brought up to efficiency. In 1809 the 25th Regiment was in Dudhope Castle, and there was an encounter betwixt the soldiers and the people, which was thus described in the "Dundee Advertiser":

> In the evening an affray took place which arose from the breaking of the head of a drum belonging to a recruiting party of the 25th Regiment of Foot. The

Fair is commonly closed with a battle; and it is so generally expected that sticks and bludgeons are prepared either for attack or defence. This trifling dispute about the drum-head was the signal for hostilities, and a battle ensued. Some artillery soldiers took one side, and the 25th Foot the other, and used swords and bayonets, and the populace stones. A young man was struck so violently with a stone that though he had strength to go home, he expired the following morning.

The soldiers did not escape scathless, for two of them were carried from the field in a state of unconsciousness, covered with wounds. In those days the Town Council employed street-porters to assist them in keeping order at the Fair, and one of these "had his skull cleft with a sword." Despite the mischief done on this occasion, no one was apprehended, and the Fair continued to have an evil reputation for lawlessness. In 1814, the "Dundee Advertiser" reports that "This Fair has always concluded with a list of broken heads, and too frequently with a list of killed and wounded."

It is an interesting fact in literary history that Tom Hood, the poet, who sang "The Song of the Shirt," witnessed the affray at Stobs Muir in 1814, and wrote a poetical description of it in his rhymed Guide to Dundee, which is quoted by Alexander Elliot in his volume on "Hood in Scotland." The passage reads thus:

> Some large markets for cattle, or Fairs, are held here,
> On a moor near the town, about thrice in the year.
> So I went to the last, found it full, to my thinking,
> Of whiskey and porter, of smoking and drinking.
> But to picture the scene these presented, indeed,
> The bold pencil and touches of Hogarth would need.
> Here you'd p'raps see a man upon quarrelling bent,
> In short serpentine curves, wheeling out of a tent
> (For at least so they call blankets raised upon poles,
> Well enlightened and aired by the numerous holes),
> Or some hobbling old wife, just as drunk as a sow,
> Having spent all the money she got for a cow,
> P'raps some yet unsold, when the market has ceased,
> You may then see a novelty—beast leading beast!

From the quotations already given from the local newspaper, it is evident that Hood's description was not exaggerated. No reform was visible for many years afterwards. In 1823 the "Dundee Advertiser" records that "the Fair sustains its ancient character for drinking, rioting, and mischief. Twelve constables were despatched by the Magistrates, but they had little effect in restraining the turbulent."

In 1824 a melancholy tragedy took place at Stobs Muir, the result of the riotous conduct of some men attending the Fair. About nine o'clock at night nine young men, masons, who had been working at Duntrune, came by appointment to Stobs Fair to meet Mr. Scott, their employer, so that they might receive their wages. After the money was paid, two of the men convoyed Mr. Scott off the Fair ground.

The other seven went towards the Stobs Toll-house, which, in accordance with custom, was "licensed to retail beer, spirits, and ale," intending to have some refreshment and to wait for their two comrades. They were refused admittance to the Toll-house, and were turning away, when a band of fourteen infuriated men rushed out of the house, armed with clubs and a hatchet, and set upon the seven poor masons. John Allan, one of these unoffending men, was felled to the earth by repeated blows, and killed on the spot. His brother ran forward to raise the lifeless body, but he also was knocked down, and though he twice arose, he was laid prostrate and bleeding. His companions were all more or less injured.

The assailants, having found that they had attacked the wrong persons, ran off to another part of Stobs Muir in search of the object of their vengeance. Here they attacked a ploughman with bludgeons, and injured him so severely that his life was despaired of, though ultimately he recovered. Turning towards the bleachfield, these ruffians set upon one of the men employed there, and rendered him unconscious.

The miscreants then dispersed, and though diligent search was made for them during the succeeding six weeks, they were never discovered. The murdered John Allan was buried in the Howff, his wounded brother walking between two supporters in the procession ; and it is recorded that "the stairs and windows were lined with sympathetic spectators as the funeral moved through the streets to the burying-ground."

This sad catastrophe seems to have brought about a complete reformation in the conduct of those attending Stobs Fair.